Student Book

ignite
English

1

Jill Carter

Christopher Edge

Peter Ellison

Liz Hanton

Martin Phillips

Alison Smith

Consultant

Geoff Barton

OXFORD

UNIVERSITY PRESS

OXFORD
UNIVERSITY PRESS

Great Clarendon Street, Oxford, OX2 6DP, United Kingdom

Oxford University Press is a department of the University of Oxford. It furthers the University's objective of excellence in research, scholarship, and education by publishing worldwide. Oxford is a registered trade mark of Oxford University Press in the UK and in certain other countries

© Oxford University Press 2014

First published in 2014

All rights reserved. No part of this publication may be reproduced, stored in a retrieval system, or transmitted, in any form or by any means, without the prior permission in writing of Oxford University Press, or as expressly permitted by law, by licence or under terms agreed with the appropriate reprographics rights organization. Enquiries concerning reproduction outside the scope of the above should be sent to the Rights Department, Oxford University Press, at the address above.

You must not circulate this work in any other form and you must impose this same condition on any acquirer

British Library Cataloguing in Publication Data

Data available

978-0-19-839242-2

10 9

Paper used in the production of this book is a natural, recyclable product made from wood grown in sustainable forests.
The manufacturing process conforms to the environmental regulations of the country of origin.

Printed in China by Golden Cup

Acknowledgements
The publishers would like to thank the following for permissions to use their photographs:

Cover: Neale Cousland/Shutterstock; **p2–3:** Luciano Mortula/Shutterstock; **p2–3:** SergeyIT/Shutterstock; **p2–3:** Susan Law Cain/Shutterstock; **p2:** sharpner/Shutterstock; **p2:** Aaron Amat/Shutterstock; **p2:** Andrey Eremin/Shutterstock; **p2:** Dwaschnig/Shutterstock; **p2:** Georgios Kollidas/Shutterstock; **p2:** Ljupco Smokovski/Shutterstock; **p2:** Montagu Images/Alamy; **p2:** Elena Kharichkina/Shutterstock; **p2:** nikkytok/Shutterstock; **p2:** rangizzz/Shutterstock; **p2:** ronstik/Shutterstock; **p2:** Rtimages/Shutterstock; **p3:** maximimages.com/Alamy; **p9:** Twitter Inc.; **p3: p10–11:** easaab/Shutterstock; **p10–11:** Jim David/Shutterstock; **p10–11:** karamysh/Shutterstock; **p10:** Aleksandr Sulga/Shutterstock; **p10:** hxdbzxy/Shutterstock; **p10:** KatarinaF/Shutterstock; **p10:** rudall30/Shutterstock; **p11:** Orfeev/Shutterstock; **p11:** Rostislav Ageev/Shutterstock; **p12:** Photos 12/Alamy; **p13:** 2j architecture/Shutterstock; **p13:** 2j architecture/Shutterstock; **p13:** Heritage Image Partnership Ltd/Alamy; **p14–15:** doughoughton/Alamy; **p14–15:** Skylines/Shutterstock; **p14:** Photos 12/Alamy; **p16–17:** Huston Brady/Shutterstock; **p16–17:** Huston Brady/Shutterstock; **p16–17:** rangizzz/Shutterstock; **p17:** Used by permission of Cartoon Books/Jeff Smith; **p18–19:** Matt Berger/Shutterstock; **p18–19:** Lonely/Shutterstock; **p19:** Roberto Caucino/Shutterstock; **p20–21:** Ozerov Alexander/Shutterstock; **p20:** Kletr/Shutterstock; **p22–23:** Iakov Kalinin/Shutterstock; **p22:** Jason Patrick Ross/Shutterstock; **p24–25:** Sergej Razvodovskij/Shutterstock; **p24–25:** STILLFX/Shutterstock; **p24–25:** SuperStock/Alamy; **p24:** Pearlimage/Alamy; **p26–27:** Archive Pics/Alamy; **p26–27:** Denis Burdin/Shutterstock; **p26–27:** Sergey Tarasenko/Shutterstock; **p26–27:** Tanchic/Shutterstock; **p28–29:** iurii/Shutterstock; **p28:** eddtoro/Shutterstock; **p30–31:** Krivosheev Vitaly/Shutterstock; **p30–31:** Napat/Shutterstock; **p30:** Oleksandr Lysenko/Shutterstock; **p30:** Sue McDonald/Shutterstock; **p32–33:** Christian Draghici/Shutterstock; **p32–33:** isaxar/Shutterstock.com; **p32–33:** marcovarro/Shutterstock.com; **p32–33:** Mike Treglia/Shutterstock; **p32–33:** Tyler Olson/Shutterstock; **p33:** sbarabu/Shutterstock; **p34–35:** xpixel/Shutterstock; **p38–40:** NFG; **p40–41:** Ben Molyneux/Alamy; **p42:** Nicku/Shutterstock; **p43:** Dan Kosmayer/Shutterstock; **p44:** JHershPhoto/Shutterstock; **p46–47:** NASA/ESA; **p46–47:** Stocktrek Images, Inc./Alamy; **p46:** Artisticco/Shutterstock; **p48–49:** Yoko Design/Shutterstock; **p50–51:** homydesign/Shutterstock; **p50–51:** hxdbzxy/Shutterstock; **p53:** DEA/G. DAGLI ORTI/Getty Images; **p55:** Natalia Klenova/Shutterstock; **p56–57:** Markus Gann/Shutterstock; **p56:** Nitiwa/Shutterstock; **p57:** Melica/Shutterstock; **p58–59:** Dominic Robinson/Flickr; **p60–61:** Stephen Coburn/Shutterstock; **p60:** NASA; **p62:** Vadelma/Shutterstock; **p64–65:** Everett Collection/Shutterstock; **p66–67:** carlos castilla/Shutterstock; **p68–69:** pixelparticle/Shutterstock; **p68–69:** Igor Zh./Shutterstock; **p68:** andrea crisante/Shutterstock; **p70:** s_bukley/Shutterstock; **p71:** anyunov/Shutterstock; **p72:** Eric Isselee/Shutterstock; **p73:** W.A. RITCHIE/ROSLIN INSTITUTE/EURELIOS/SCIENCE PHOTO LIBRARY; **p78:** Kamira/Shutterstock; **p78:** Lucian/Shutterstock; **p80–81:** Andrey Yurlov/Shutterstock; **p80:** D.C Comics 2005; **p81:** With kind permission from Neill Cameron/Phoenix Comics; **p82–83:** Gil.K/Shutterstock; **p82:** Photos 12/Alamy; **p86–87:** Aleksandar Mijatovic/Shutterstock; **p86–87:** melis/Shutterstock; **p86–87:** StockImageGroup/Shutterstock; **p86–87:** Sukharevskyy Dmytro (nevodka)/Shutterstock; **p88–89:** Radiokafka/Shutterstock; **p88:** Anna Anisimova/Shutterstock; **p90–91:** Alexey Stiop/Alamy; **p90:** ethylalkohol/Shutterstock; **p92–93:** Suzy Bennett/Alamy; **p94–95:** Smit/Shutterstock; **p94–95:** Napat/Shutterstock; **p94:** Marcus Eldh/Wild Sweden; **p95:** Brocreative/Shutterstock; **p96:** D. Kucharski K. Kucharska/Shutterstock; **p97:** 1000 Words/Shutterstock.com; **p98–99:** samarttiw/Shutterstock; **p98–99:** Lynn Amaral/Shutterstock; **p98:** K. Miri Photography/Shutterstock; **p100–101:** Iakov Filimonov/Shutterstock; **p100–101:** kyu/Shutterstock; **p100–101:** wong yu liang/Shutterstock; **p100–101:** arka38/Shutterstock; **p102–103:** North Wind Picture Archives/Alamy; **p104–105:** photo25th/Shutterstock; **p104–105:** Pabkov/Shutterstock; **p104:** cosma/Shutterstock; **p104:** Jiri Hera/Shutterstock; **p104:** Refat/Shutterstock; **p104:** rvlsoft/Shutterstock; **p104:** Aleksandar Mijatovic/Shutterstock; **p105:** CHEN HENG KONG/Shutterstock; **p105:** Kamira/Shutterstock; **p105:** Neyro/Shutterstock; **p105:** Valesca Hogeboom/Shutterstock; **p105:** aragami12345s/Shutterstock; **p105:** Dimedrol68/Shutterstock; **p105:** PinkBlue/Shutterstock; **p106–107:** Stephen Marques/Shutterstock; **p106:** Ljupco Smokovski/Shutterstock; **p106:** ronstik/Shutterstock; **p106:** Ian Canham/Alamy; **p106:** maximimages.com/Alamy; **p106:** PRILL/Shutterstock; **p106:** rangizzz/Shutterstock; **p106:** REX/Ken McKay; **p107:** jordeangjelovik/Shutterstock; **p107:** rvlsoft/Shutterstock; **p108:** Jeff Gilbert/Alamy; **p108:** withGod/Shutterstock; **p109:** Ian Canham/Alamy; **p109:** Kapreski/Shutterstock; **p109:** Wiktoria Pawlak/Shutterstock; **p110:** REX/Ken McKay; **p113:** Julia Ivantsova/Shutterstock; **p114–115:** Vacheslav Votchicev/Alamy; **p114–115:** withGod/Shutterstock; **p116:** Gerry Ellis/Minden Pictures/Corbis; **p116:** JanP/Alamy; **p117:** AFP/Getty Images; **p118–119:** keren-seg/Shutterstock; **p118:** Hauke Dressler/Getty Images; **p118:** Mark III Photonics/Shutterstok; **p119:** Tyler Olson/Shutterstock; **p119:** wavebreakmedia/Shutterstock; **p120–121:** calvindexter/Shutterstock; **p120:** Jeff Overs/BBC News; **p120:** Jeff Overs/BBC News; **p120:** Tara Moore/Corbis; **p122–123:** Jeff Gilbert/Alamy; **p124–125:** DeshaCAM/Shutterstock; **p126–127:** alanf/Shutterstock; **p127:** IvicaNS/Shutterstock; **p127:** Hugh Ryono/Aquarium of the Pacific; **p128–129:** ESA/P.Carril; **p128:** MarcelClemens/Shutterstock; **pg129:** Gl0ck/Shutterstock **p130–131:** withGod/Shutterstock; **p130:** maximimages.com/Alamy; **p131:** Ian Canham/Alamy; **p131:** Ian Canham/Alamy; **p132–133:** Kvadrat/Shutterstock; **p132:** ComZeal/Shutterstock; **p134:** johnfoto18/Shutterstock; **p134:** Paul Vidler/Alamy; **p138–139:** Capture Light/Shutterstock; **p138–139:** Elena Schweitzer/Shutterstock; **p140–141:** Helene Rogers/Alamy; **p144–145:** Andrey_Kuzmin/Shutterstock; **p144–145:** joingate/Shutterstock; **p144–145:** Miguel Angel Salinas Salinas/Shutterstock; p**148–149:** Renata Sedmakova/Shutterstock; **p151:** Complot/Shutterstock; **p153:** Georgios Kollidas/Shutterstock; **p156–157:** antpkr/Shutterstock; **p156–157:** ronstik/Shutterstock

Illustrations on p135 by Nick Harris. All other images by New Future Graphic.
The authors and publisher are grateful for permission to reprint extracts from the following copyright material:

Her Majesty The Queen's Christmas message 2012 is Crown © copyright and is reprinted by permission of Buckingham Palace.

Alison Allen-Gray: *Unique* (OUP, 2009), copyright © Alison Allen-Gray 2009, reprinted by permission of Oxford University Press.

Isaac Asimov: 'The Three Laws of Robotics' from *I Robot* (Voyager, 2001), copyright © Isaac Asimov 1950, and 'True Love' in *The Complete Robot* (Voyager, 1996), copyright © Isaac Asimov 1982, reprinted by permission of HarperCollins Publishers Ltd.

Pam Ayres: 'Oh, I Wish I'd Looked After Me Teeth' from *The Works: The Classic Collection* (BBC Books, 2008), copyright © Pam Ayres 1992, 2008, reprinted by permission of Sheil Land Associates Ltd.

Samantha Bangayan: Huancayo travel guide, copyright © Samantha Bangayan 2011, first published on www.howtoperu.com,1 May 2011, reprinted by permission of the author, www.whatlittlethings.com.

James Berry: 'Isn't My Name Magical?' from *Only One of Me* (Macmillan, 2004),copyright © James Berry 2004, reprinted by permission of Macmillan Publishers Ltd.

Christopher Booker: *The Seven Basic Plots: Why We Tell Stories* (Continuum, 2005), reprinted by permission of the publishers, an imprint of Bloomsbury Publishing Plc.

Elizabeth Bradfield: 'In the Polar Regions' from *Approaching Ice: Poems* (Persea/W W Norton, 2010), copyright © Elizabeth Bradfield 2010, reprinted by permission of Persea Books, Inc, New York. All rights reserved.

Julie Bretagna: *Exodus* (Young Picador, 2002), copyright © Julie Bretagna 2002, reprinted by permission of The Greenhouse Literary Agency on behalf of the author.

Gillian Cross: *Tightrope* (OUP, 2010), copyright © Gillian Cross 1999, reprinted by permission of Oxford University Press.

Russell T Davies and **Benjamin Cook:** *Doctor Who: The Writer's Tale: The Untold Story of the BBC Series* (BBC Books, 2010), reprinted by permission of The Random House Group Ltd.

Heather Dawe: *Adventures in Mind: A Personal Obsession with the Mountains* (Vertebrate Publishing, 2013), reprinted by permission of the publishers.

Julia Donaldson: *The Gruffalo*, illustrated by Axel Scheffler (Macmillan Children's Books, 1999), text copyright © Julia Donaldson 1999, reprinted by permission of Macmillan Publishers Ltd.

James Dorsey: 'My Friend Moses' copyright © James Dorsey 2012, first published on www.besttravelwriting.com, 12 March 2012, reprinted by permission of the author.

Dreadlock Alien: 'Well Done', performance poem, copyright © Richard Grant 2013, reprinted by permission of the author, Richard Grant.

Geoff Dyer: *Jeff in Venice: Death in Varanasi* (Canongate, 2009), copyright © Geoff Dyer 2009, reprinted by permission of Canongate Books Ltd.

Ross Fraser: 'Your Guide to Eating Insects in Bangkok' published on www.travelwithamate.com, reprinted by permission of the publishers, Preston Creative Partnership.

Robert Frost: 'The Road Not Taken' from *The Poetry of Robert Frost* edited by Edward Connery Lathem (Cape, 1971), reprinted by permission of The Random House Group Ltd.

Damien Gayle: 'Rise of the Machines: Autonomous killer robots could be developed in 20 years *The Mail Online*, 20.11.2012, copyright © Associated Newspapers 2012, reprinted by permission of Solo Syndication for the *Daily Mail*.

Sophie Hannah: 'Differences' from *Selected Poems* (Penguin, 2006), copyright © Sophie Hannah 2006, reprinted by permission of the author.

Rob Harris: 'How to be,...Samira Ahmed; TV News Presenter', *The Guardian*, 14.3.2005, copyright © Guardian News and Media Ltd 2005, reprinted by permission of GNM Ltd.

Seamus Heaney: 'Scaffolding' from *Death of a Naturalist* (Faber, 1966), reprinted by permission of Faber & Faber.

Mandy Huggins: 'Tales from the Edge of the Sahara', copyright © Mandy Huggins 2012, from troutiemcfishtales.blogspot.co.uk, 4.4.2012.

Simon Jenkins: 'From Greenland to Mount Everest, this is the season of reckless jaunts', *The Guardian*, 2.5.2013, copyright © Guardian News and Media Ltd 2013, reprinted by permission of GNM Ltd.

Lucy Jordan: 'Brasil Zoo to clone endangered species', *The Rio Times*, 18.11.2012, reprinted by permission of The Brazil News Agency, Inc.

Laurie Lee: *Cider with Rosie* (Penguin, 1998), copyright © Laurie Lee 1959, reprinted by permission of Curtis Brown Group Ltd, London on behalf of The Estate of Laurie Lee.

Sir John Mandeville, translated by C W R D Moseley: *The Travels of Sir John Mandeville* (Penguin Classics, 2005), translation copyright © C W R D Moseley 1983, reprinted by permission of Penguin Books Ltd.

R J Palacio: *Wonder* (David Fickling Books, 2012), reprinted by permission of The Random House Group Ltd.

Elise Paschen: 'Birth' from *Bestiary* (Red Hen Press, 2009), copyright © Elise Paschen 2009, reprinted by permission of the publishers.

Terry Pratchett: *Nation* (Doubleday, 2009), copyright © Terry Pratchett 2009, reprinted by permission of The Random House Publishing Group Ltd.

Mark Prigg: 'P-p-p-pick up an iPad: Zoo unveils latest treat for penguins - an app they play with their beak', *Daily Mail*, 18.3.2013, copyright © Associated Newspapers 2013, reprinted by permission of Solo Syndication for the *Daily Mail*.

Philip Reeve: *Mortal Engines* (Scholastic, 2001), copyright © Philip Reeve 2001, reproduced by permission of Scholastic Ltd. All rights reserved.

Dave Robson: 'Middlesbrough school urges parents to correct pupils' Tees dialect', from *Gazette Live*, 5.2.2013, reprinted by permission of Newcastle Syndication for the *Middlesborough Evening Gazette*, Trinity Mirror Publishing Ltd.

Kira Salak: *Four Corners: A Journey into the Heart of Papua New Guinea* (National Geographic Books, 2004), reprinted by permission of the author.

Joe Simpson: *The Beckoning Silence* (Jonathan Cape, 2002) reprinted by permission of The Random House Group Ltd and the author.

Kate Tempest: 'Cannibal Kids' from *Everything Speaks in its Own Way* (Zingaro Books, 2012), copyright © Kate Tempest 2012, reprinted by permission of Fox Mason on behalf of the author.

Paul Theroux: *The Old Patagonian Express* (Penguin, 2008), copyright © Paul Theroux 1979, 2008, reprinted by permission of The Wylie Agency (UK) Ltd.

Dylan Thomas: 'The Outing' from *A Dylan Thomas Treasury* (J M Dent, 1991), reprinted by permission of David Higham Associates.

J R R Tolkien: *The Hobbit* (HarperCollins, 2012) , copyright © The J R R Tolkien Estate Ltd 1937, 1965, reprinted by permission of HarperCollins Publishers Ltd.

Alice Walker: 'Poem at Thirty-Nine' from *Collected Poems 1965-1990* (Phoenix, 2005), copyright © Alice Walker 1991, reprinted by permission of David Higham Associates.

Benjamin Zephaniah: 'The British' from *Wicked World* (Puffin, 2000), copyright © Benjamin Zephaniah 2000, reprinted by permission of Penguin Books Ltd.

and to the following for their permission to reprint extracts from copyright material:

Compassion in World Farming (CIWF) for "Cloning = Cruelty" from www.ciwf.org.uk.

Little Brown Book Group Ltd for back cover blurb for *Contact* by Carl Sagan (Orbit Books, 1997).

Oxford University Press for back cover blurb for *The Invisible Man* by H G Wells adapted by Adrian Flynn (Oxford Playscripts, OUP, 2012).

Penguin Books Ltd for cover blurb for John Wyndham: *The Day of the Triffids* (Penguin Classics, 2000 edition)

Swedish Tourist Board (Svenska Turistföreningen) for extract and photograph of 'Sweden's Most Primitive Hotel', photo © Skogens Konung, from www.svenskaturistforeningen.se.

Although we have made every effort to trace and contact all copyright holders before publication this has not been possible in all cases. If notified, the publisher will rectify any errors or omissions at the earliest opportunity.

Links to third party websites are provided by Oxford in good faith and for information only. Oxford disclaims any responsibility for the materials contained in any third party website referenced in this work.

Ignite English has been written by people who love teaching English. It was a pre-requisite for us when developing this resource that you have people who are confident teaching English and who would find it patronizing to tell you how to teach English. Therefore we have provided a flexibility, both digitally and on the page, so that you can decide how you are going to customize it for your students.

In *Ignite English*, we also take English and show how it relates to the real world. Outside school there are lots of people doing lots of different jobs who will be using speaking, listening, reading and writing and we might not even think about how they are doing it. Well let's! In *Ignite English*, we take a look at what they do and we talk to them about how they are doing it, so that you and your students can explore the way they are using language and connect what we are doing in the classroom with the world out there.

Informed by research and recent Ofsted reports, *Ignite English* aims to help reinvigorate KS3 English teaching and learning by:

- Improving learning through relevance and creativity
- Ensuring teaching is distinctive
- Enabling effective transition between Year 6 and Year 7
- Accessing up-to-date and relevant professional development
- Delivering the new KS3 National Curriculum

That is essentially what we are trying to do with *Ignite English*.

Geoff Barton

Series Consultant, Head Teacher, Teacher of English and highly experienced English author

Ignite English authors

Ignite English was created with Geoff Barton and authored by experienced teachers and educationalists who are passionate about teaching English. As well as being tested in schools and reviewed by teachers, the resources were also reviewed by Peter Ellison, a cross-phase Local Authority Adviser and Phil Jarrett, former Ofsted National Adviser for English.

Contents

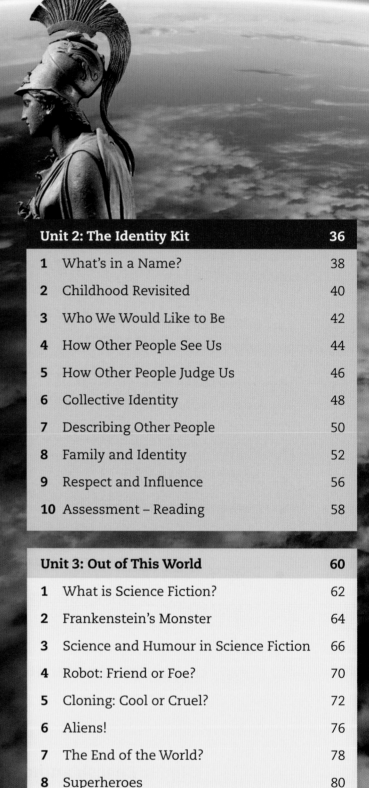

| Overview of *Ignite English* | 6 |
| Introduction to English: What is English? | 8 |

Unit 1: In Search of Adventure — 10

1	The Hero's Journey	12
2	The Call to Adventure	14
3	Comic-book Heroes	16
4	Polar Explorers	18
5	Unexpected Encounters	20
6	Survival Skills	24
7	At the Extremes	26
8	Worth the Risk?	30
9	Assessment – Reading	32

Unit 2: The Identity Kit — 36

1	What's in a Name?	38
2	Childhood Revisited	40
3	Who We Would Like to Be	42
4	How Other People See Us	44
5	How Other People Judge Us	46
6	Collective Identity	48
7	Describing Other People	50
8	Family and Identity	52
9	Respect and Influence	56
10	Assessment – Reading	58

Unit 3: Out of This World — 60

1	What is Science Fiction?	62
2	Frankenstein's Monster	64
3	Science and Humour in Science Fiction	66
4	Robot: Friend or Foe?	70
5	Cloning: Cool or Cruel?	72
6	Aliens!	76
7	The End of the World?	78
8	Superheroes	80
9	New Worlds	82
10	Assessment – Writing	84

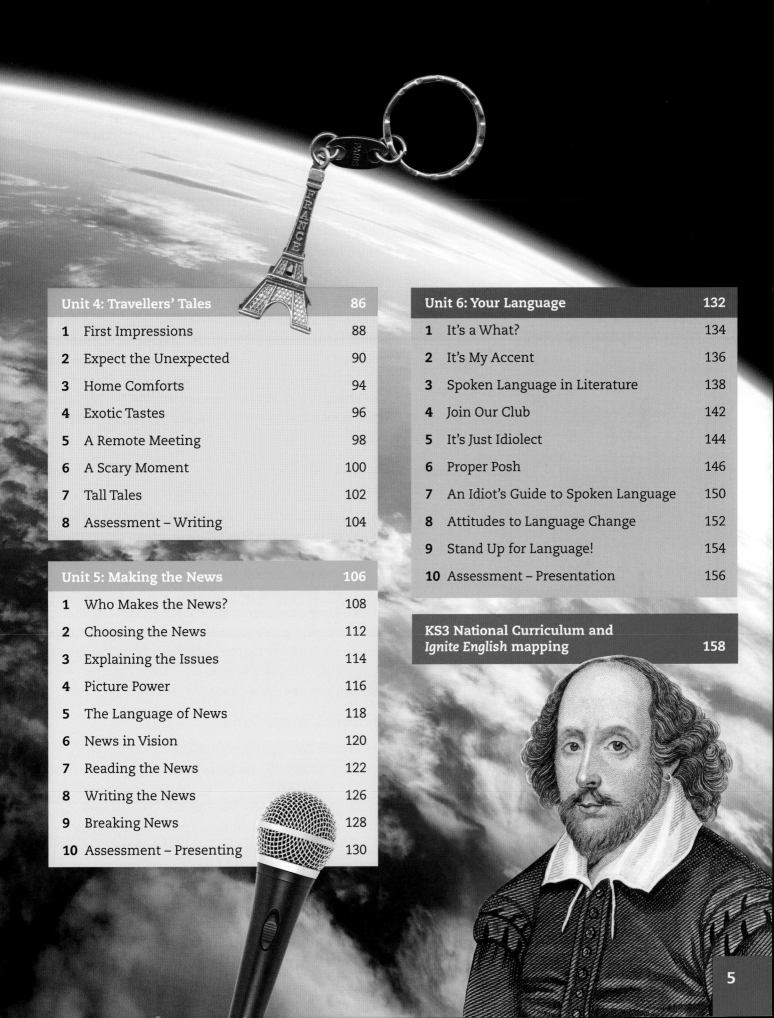

Unit 4: Travellers' Tales	86
1 First Impressions	88
2 Expect the Unexpected	90
3 Home Comforts	94
4 Exotic Tastes	96
5 A Remote Meeting	98
6 A Scary Moment	100
7 Tall Tales	102
8 Assessment – Writing	104

Unit 5: Making the News	106
1 Who Makes the News?	108
2 Choosing the News	112
3 Explaining the Issues	114
4 Picture Power	116
5 The Language of News	118
6 News in Vision	120
7 Reading the News	122
8 Writing the News	126
9 Breaking News	128
10 Assessment – Presenting	130

Unit 6: Your Language	132
1 It's a What?	134
2 It's My Accent	136
3 Spoken Language in Literature	138
4 Join Our Club	142
5 It's Just Idiolect	144
6 Proper Posh	146
7 An Idiot's Guide to Spoken Language	150
8 Attitudes to Language Change	152
9 Stand Up for Language!	154
10 Assessment – Presentation	156

KS3 National Curriculum and *Ignite English* mapping	158

Overview of *Ignite English*

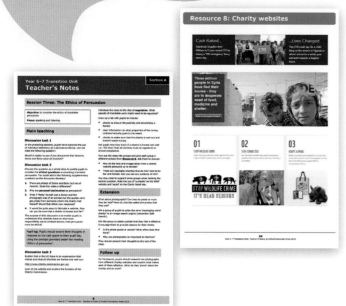

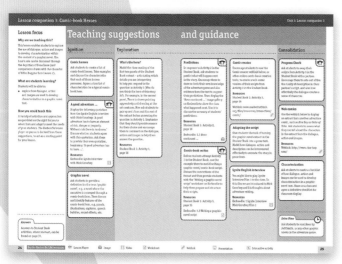

Transition support

Teacher Companion 1 includes English lesson suggestions and guidance on effective transition from Primary to Secondary school. It also includes a range of teaching ideas for the first week of English lessons in Secondary schools, with an opening lesson included in Student Book 1. In addition, there is a professional development unit specifically on transition in Kerboodle: Lessons, Resources and Assessments.

Also on Kerboodle LRA 1 and on the Oxford University Press *Ignite English* webpage, you will find a unit of work, with transition tips, for Primary school teachers to use in the final term of Year 6. This unit, 'Making a Difference', has *Ignite English* principles at its heart and we hope that by passing this unit on to local Primary schools it will foster enhanced relationships between Secondary school English departments and colleagues in local Primary schools.

Student Books

The Student Books have been designed to develop a range of reading, writing and spoken English skills in real-life contexts. Each Student Book offers thematically-focused units, covering prose fiction, poetry, drama and non-fiction forms, as well as a focus on language and one unique immersive unit based around a real-world scenario. They also feature an explicit focus on spelling, punctuation and grammar (SPAG). There is a wide range of source texts and activities with Stretch and Support as well as regular Progress Checks and Extra Time features, which can be used either for extension or homework.

Teacher Companions

Each Teacher Companion shares the thinking and philosophy behind the resources with a focus on the 'why', 'what' and 'how' of each unit, lesson and assessment. Additionally, the Teacher Companions feature unit-by-unit teaching support materials with comprehensive teaching tips, links and further reading suggestions. Each lesson features a Lesson Companion that includes a range of teaching ideas, guidance and tips to enable you to customize your lessons. The Teacher Companion also includes guidance and suggestions on setting up and marking the end of unit assessments.

Kerboodle: Lessons, Resources and Assessment

Kerboodle is packed full of guided support and ideas for creating and running effective lessons. It's intuitive to use, customizable, and can be accessed online anytime and anywhere. *Ignite English* Kerboodle LRA includes:

- 18 exclusive interviews providing over 40 unique and compelling films, connecting the learning in KS3 English lessons to skills used in thematically-linked jobs

- eight specially-commissioned filmed units providing CPD for English departments on key areas of Key Stage 3 teaching and learning, including genuine lesson footage, interviews with Primary and Secondary school teachers and students, and comments and observations from Geoff Barton and Phil Jarrett

- materials to support the transition for students from Key Stage 2 to Key Stage 3

- grammar support for teachers and students through extensive technical accuracy interactives and a grammar reference guide

- a wealth of additional resources including: interactive activities, an editable alternative end-of-unit assessment for every Student Book unit, marking scales to help monitor progress, photos, editable presentations, editable worksheets (general, differentiation and peer/self-assessment) and weblinks

- Lesson Player, enabling teachers to deliver ready-made lessons or the freedom to customize plans to suit your classes' needs.

Kerboodle Online Student Books

All three student books are also available as Online Student Books. These can be accessed on a range of devices, such as tablets, and offer a bank of tools to enable students to personalize their book and view notes left by the teacher.

Dreadlock Alien: I used up ten pencils in one day!

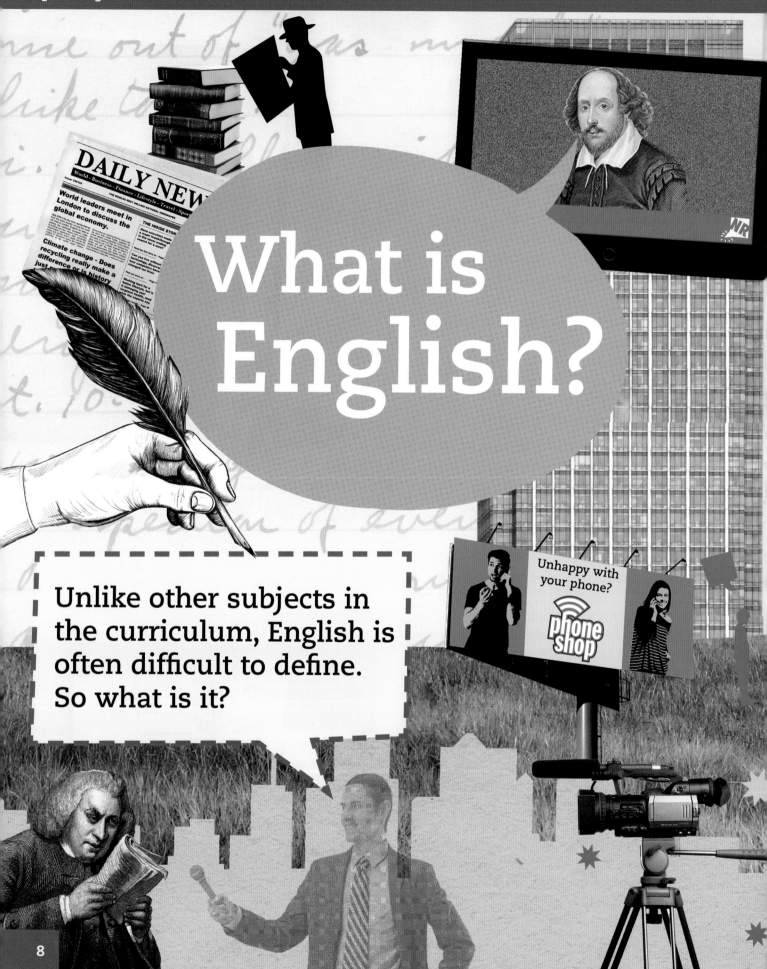

What is English?

Unlike other subjects in the curriculum, English is often difficult to define. So what is it?

Introduction

At its heart, English is about how you learn to communicate effectively with others and how you learn to understand ideas communicated to you. Communication is going on all around you, but it isn't just about what's happening now. Reading enables us to receive communications from people who may have lived centuries ago – a kind of time-travel.

In your secondary school English lessons, you will be learning how to become a more sophisticated reader, writer and speaker. You will also be learning about the thoughts and feelings of people in far off places and from previous centuries. Think of it as a journey.

Activities

1 Look at the images on page 8 and discuss how you think they might contribute to our understanding of the subject of English. What do they all have in common?

2 Think for a few minutes about all the communication that is taking place right now across the world. Consider:

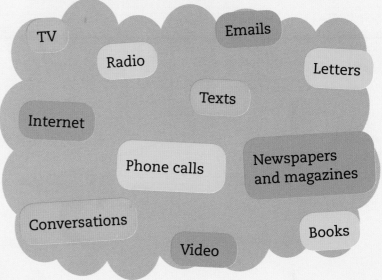

TV

Emails

Radio

Letters

Texts

Internet

Phone calls

Newspapers and magazines

Conversations

Books

Video

How many of the above list do you use every day?

3 Here is what some writers have said about reading:

'Reading is the sole means by which we slip, involuntarily, often helplessly, into another's skin, another's voice, another's soul.'
Joyce Carol Oates

'We read to know that we are not alone.'
C. S. Lewis

'Picking five favourite books is like picking the five body parts you'd most like not to lose.'
Neil Gaiman

Discuss them with a partner. What does each of these quotations say about reading?

1

IN SEARCH OF ADVENTURE

What drives people to seek out adventure?

Introduction

To go on an adventure is to journey into the unknown. From quests to slay dragons to exploring the edge of space, adventures can thrill readers as well as the people who experience them. But what drives people to seek out adventure?

In this unit, you will explore extracts from stories, poems and non-fiction writing about adventure, meeting real-life explorers as well as some famous fictional adventurers too.

ignite *INTERVIEW*

Mick Conefrey, Adventure writer and documentary maker

Adventure is exciting because we like watching and reading about things that we would like to do. I am interested in reading stories about people climbing mountains or going to extreme places, because I would like to be there. They are doing the things that I would like to do. But also there is a kind of sense that sometimes they are taking risks that I would like somebody else to take. If you look at the true stories of what has happened to people in the history of exploration, they are as extreme and as strange and as bizarre as anything you could make up.

Activities

1 What is the most adventurous thing you have ever done? This could be taking part in an adventurous sport or activity, visiting a faraway place or any other daring experience.

2 Discuss how you felt before, during and after the experience. Why do you think people seek out adventure?

1 The Hero's Journey

↺ Objective

Explore the typical structure of adventure stories and relate this to your own reading.

Whether they are found in books or films, adventure stories often follow a similar structure, which is sometimes known as the hero's journey.

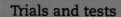

The hero's journey

The call to adventure

The hero or heroine receives a challenge that will take them away from their ordinary life, for example, a quest to follow or a dangerous mission to complete.

Into the unknown

The hero or heroine sets out on their adventure, entering a new world filled with dangers.

Trials and tests

On the path to their final goal, the hero or heroine encounters difficult obstacles that they have to overcome.

The final challenge

The hero or heroine faces their greatest challenge and must endure an ordeal to achieve the aim of their adventure.

Reward and return

The hero or heroine receives some form of reward and returns a changed person.

✎ Activities

1 Discuss whether the adventure stories you have read or watched follow this structure. Why do you think this might be?

2 Create your own flow diagram, adding examples for each stage from books and films you have read or seen.

Now read the extract below where the writer, Christopher Booker, describes the plot of the earliest ever adventure story, the *Epic of Gilgamesh*, an ancient poem written over 5000 years ago.

3 Find any similarities between the plot of the *Epic of Gilgamesh* and adventure stories you have watched or read, e.g. James Bond, *The Lord of the Rings*, etc.

Extract from *The Seven Basic Plots: Why We Tell Stories* by Christopher Booker

The first part of the **Sumerian** *Epic of Gilgamesh*, as we now know it, tells of how the kingdom of Uruk has fallen under the terrible shadow of a great and mysterious evil. The source of the threat is traced to a monstrous figure, Humbaba, who lives half across the world, at the heart of a remote forest. The hero, Gilgamesh, goes to the armourers who equip him with special weapons, a great bow and a mighty axe. He sets out on a long, hazardous journey to Humbaba's distant lair, where he finally comes face to face with the monster. They enjoy a series of **taunting exchanges**, then embark on a **titanic** struggle. Against such supernatural powers, it seems Gilgamesh cannot possibly win. But finally, by a superhuman feat, he manages to kill his monstrous opponent. The shadowy threat has been lifted. Gilgamesh has saved his kingdom and can return home triumphant...

4 Write two paragraphs comparing the structure of two adventure stories you have read or watched. Use conjunctions to help you draw out interesting comparisons and contrasts between the stories.

SPAG

Conjunctions link different parts of a sentence. There are two main types of conjunction:

* A coordinating conjunction links two independent clauses in a sentence, e.g. *The Epic of Gilgamesh was written over 5000 years ago* **but** *Dr No is a 20th-century James Bond story.*

* A subordinate conjunction introduces a **subordinate clause** in a sentence, e.g. **While** *James Bond might be more famous, Gilgamesh is the original hero.*

📖 Glossary

Sumerian   belonging to Sumer, an ancient kingdom located in modern-day Iraq

taunting exchanges   insults and gibes

titanic   colossal

subordinate clause   a clause that supports the main clause in giving further explanation or detail, but cannot stand alone. It may start with words such as 'which', 'who', 'that' or 'when'.

2 The Call to Adventure

↻ Objective

Investigate how a writer builds up expectations of an adventure story through character and **setting**.

At the beginning of an adventure story, something must happen that pulls the hero or heroine out of their everyday life and plunges them into an adventure. In the extract from the opening chapter of J. R. R. Tolkien's novel *The Hobbit* on page 15, Bilbo Baggins is standing outside his home when he sees a stranger approaching. Read the extract and then complete the activities.

✎ Activities

1 Tolkien uses description and **dialogue** to introduce Gandalf to the reader. Discuss what you learn about the character from:

- the way Tolkien describes his appearance
- the way he speaks and what he says.

2 What impression do you get of Bilbo Baggins from this extract? Think about:

- what he says
- how he acts
- what he thinks.

3 Bilbo describes adventures as 'Nasty disturbing uncomfortable things!' that 'Make you late for dinner!' Discuss why you think Tolkien has chosen to make Bilbo the hero of this story.

4 SPAG What do you notice about the punctuation in this extract? Pick out some examples and comment on the effect that they have.

Extract from *The Hobbit* by J. R. R. Tolkien

All that the unsuspecting Bilbo saw that morning was an old man with a **staff**. He had a tall pointed blue hat, a long grey cloak, a silver scarf over which his long white beard hung down below his waist, and immense black boots.

"Good morning!" said Bilbo, and he meant it. The sun was shining, and the grass was very green. But Gandalf looked at him from under long bushy eyebrows that stuck out further than the brim of his shady hat.

"What do you mean?" he said. "Do you wish me a good morning, or mean that it is a good morning whether I want it or not; or that you feel good this morning; or that it is a morning to be good on?"

"All of them at once," said Bilbo. "And a very fine morning for a pipe of tobacco out of doors, into the bargain. If you have a pipe about you, sit down and have a fill of mine! There's no hurry, we have all the day before us!" Then Bilbo sat down on a seat by his door, crossed his legs, and blew out a beautiful grey ring of smoke that sailed up into the air without breaking and floated away over The Hill.

"Very pretty!" said Gandalf. "But I have no time to blow smoke-rings this morning. I am looking for someone to share in an adventure that I am arranging, and it's very difficult to find anyone."

"I should think so – in these parts! We are plain quiet folk and have no use for adventures. Nasty disturbing uncomfortable things! Make you late for dinner! I can't think what anybody sees in them," said our Mr Baggins, and stuck one thumb behind his braces, and blew out another even bigger smoke-ring. Then he took out his morning letters, and began to read, pretending to take no more notice of the old man. He had decided that he was not quite his sort, and wanted him to go away.

📖 Glossary

setting the place and time where the novel occurs

dialogue conversation between two or more characters

staff a long walking stick

☑ Progress Check

Produce a list of tips about how to use dialogue, action, description and punctuation to create an effective opening for an adventure story.

🕐 Extra Time

Read more of *The Hobbit* or other adventure stories by J. R. R. Tolkien.

3 Comic-book Heroes

↻ Objective

Explore how dialogue, action and images are used to develop characterization in a graphic novel text.

Adventure stories are often found in comic books and graphic novels. Here, writers and illustrators use pictures as well as words to tell the story. In the extract from Jeff Smith's graphic novel *Bone* on page 17, Fone Bone and his friend Thorn are lost in the forest and surrounded by menacing rat creatures.

✎ Activities

1 Who do you think the hero of this story is? Give reasons for your choice based on the extract.

📚 Support

Look closely at how Fone Bone and Thorn are depicted, e.g. their actions, facial expressions and dialogue. Think about what these suggest about each character.

2 Drawing on your knowledge of adventure stories, discuss what you think will happen next in the story. Think about:

- what Fone Bone and Thorn might do
- how the rat creatures might react
- any other characters who might appear.

3 Create a script for the next page of the graphic novel. Use description and dialogue to show how the action develops.

Description: Thorn clasps Fone Bone protectively with one arm, while she points aggressively towards the rat creatures with her other free hand. The expression on her face is angry and defiant, while Fone Bone looks scared.

Dialogue: STAY BACK!

Sound effects: SSSSS---

↔ Stretch

Think about the ways you can change the characterization of Fone Bone. Experiment with different captions and dialogue to make him either a brave or reluctant adventurer.

4 Polar Explorers

 Objective

Understand how Elizabeth Bradfield conveys the dangers of exploration in her poem 'In the Polar Regions'.

What dangers lay in wait for the very first explorers who sought to conquer the harsh environment of Antarctica? Read Elizabeth Bradfield's poem 'In the Polar Regions' on page 19 and then complete the activities.

Activities

1 What do you think this poem is about? Share your ideas about the poem. Pick out details that you don't understand on first reading and discuss what these might mean.

Support

Some words and lines in poetry have more than one meaning. For instance, what different possible meanings might there be for the following lines?

'It takes a particular man for this, you know, able to be short-sighted for months on end.'

2 This poem is about the very first Antarctic explorers. What picture does Elizabeth Bradfield create of the difficulties and dangers of polar exploration at this time? Think about:

- who the narrator of the poem is and how Bradfield creates their voice
- what she suggests about the dangers and discomforts faced by polar explorers
- her use of imagery, including **metaphor** and **extended metaphor**.

3 Create a dramatic reading of the poem to teach other Year 7 students about the extreme experiences of some adventurers. Think about how you can use **intonation** and **tone** to communicate the emotions you want to evoke.

Stretch

Think about how you could use dramatic techniques such as tableaux (freeze frame) to accompany your reading of the poem.

☑ Progress Check

Perform your dramatic reading in front of the class. Ask them to give you a rating, on a scale of 1 to 5, with 5 being the highest, on how effectively you used intonation and tone to evoke the emotions of the poem.

'In the Polar Regions' by Elizabeth Bradfield

Long from home. Glaciers capping the hills
like false teeth. It's not just the odd meat
we're carving, clawed flippers and flightless
wings, or the long-churned distance to any news of home,
any first-born or failing parent. There
are other signs this place is foreign. The ship
converses with ice packed around it, groans
and squeaks, an occasional outraged crack.

It takes a particular man for this, you know,
able to be short-sighted for months on end.
The air is constantly **aluminum** with snow,
and my mouth, too, tastes of metal. Salt
of iron seeping from my weakened gums.
Each morning, I pack drift around my tongue
to freeze the soft flesh holding my teeth.

It all goes to slush—ground underneath
our tents, my mouth, the knack for conversation.
Walking west, five of us have fallen
to dangle alongside cliffs of ice, the thin crust
breaking into chasm easily, as if such sudden transformations
were to be expected and we're the fools to be surprised.
Only a thin rope holds us to the surface. Hanging,
there's nothing to do but stare at the blue contours of freeze
and tongue our loosening teeth, test the stringy roots
that hold them, wait for a tug from the ones left above.

📖 Glossary

metaphor describing something as something else, not meant to be taken literally, e.g. *You are a star.*

extended metaphor continuing the use of the metaphor throughout the whole text or a number of lines

intonation the rise and fall of a person's voice when they speak

tone the way words are spoken, e.g. a serious tone, a light-hearted tone, etc.

aluminum American spelling of aluminium

5 Unexpected Encounters

↻ Objective

Examine how features of writing can be used to create suspense and tension in an adventure story.

One of the first novels written in English was *Robinson Crusoe* by Daniel Defoe. This adventure story tells the tale of a sailor, Robinson Crusoe, who is shipwrecked and cast away on a deserted island. In the extract on page 21, Crusoe is walking along the beach when he encounters an unexpected sight.

✎ Activities

1 What does Crusoe see and why does this surprise him? Discuss how you think you would react in his situation.

2 How does Defoe show Crusoe's changing reactions? Pick out details from the extract and explain what they show about Crusoe's emotions.

SPAG

3 How does the way the sentences are constructed help you to build up a picture of Crusoe's thoughts and actions? Explore how:

- commas are used to separate subordinate clauses
- conjunctions and semi-colons are used to link ideas
- the punctuation reflects Crusoe's thoughts and actions.

Extract from *Robinson Crusoe* by Daniel Defoe

It happened one day, about noon, going towards my boat, I was exceedingly surprised with the print of a man's naked foot on the shore, which was very plain to be seen on the sand. I stood like one thunderstruck, or as if I had seen an **apparition**. I listened, I looked round me, I could hear nothing, nor see anything; I went up to a rising ground to look farther; I went up the shore and down the shore, but it was all one; I could see no other impression but that one. I went to it again to see if there were any more, and to observe if it might not be my fancy; but there was no room for that, for there was exactly the print of a foot – toes, heel, and every part of a foot. How it came **thither** I knew not, nor could in the least imagine; but after innumerable fluttering thoughts, like a man perfectly confused and out of myself, I came home to my **fortification**, not feeling, as we say, the ground I went on, but terrified to the last degree, looking behind me at every two or three steps, mistaking every bush and tree, and fancying every stump at a distance to be a man. Nor is it possible to describe how many various shapes my affrighted imagination represented things to me in, how many wild ideas were found every moment in my fancy, and what strange, unaccountable **whimsies** came into my thoughts by the way.

📖 Glossary

apparition   ghost

thither   to that place

fortification   fort

whimsies   freakish ideas

Now read the extract from *Nation* by Terry Pratchett on pages 22–23. This tells the story of another castaway who is shipwrecked on a desert island, but this extract is told from the perspective of an islander, a boy called Mau.

4 Compare and contrast the ways the two extracts create a sense of tension. Look at:

SPAG

- the events of the extracts
- the thoughts and actions of the characters
- the way punctuation and paragraphs are used.

5 Continue the extract from *Robinson Crusoe*. Think about:

- what might happen next in the story, e.g. Crusoe meeting the person who has left the footprint
- the different sentence structures you can use to create tension and suspense
- how you can use paragraphs to show the sequence of events and add impact.

↔ Stretch

For Activity 5, try writing in the style of Terry Pratchett's *Nation*.

🕐 Extra Time

Find out more about *Robinson Crusoe* and the real-life events that inspired the story.

More to explore

Extract from *Nation* **by Terry Pratchett**

Mau peered round the **buttress** of a giant fig tree.

There was a lot to see.

Something had been wrecked, but it was not alive. It was some kind of giant canoe, stuck between the trunks of two trees and covered with debris that looked as though it would be worth investigating, but not now. A big hole in the side leaked stones. But all this was background. Much closer to Mau, and staring at him in horror, was a girl – probably. But she could be a ghost; she was very pale.

And a **trouserman**, too. The trousers were white and frilly, like the feathery legs of a grandfather bird, but she also had some kind of skirt tucked up around her waist. And her hair glowed in the sunlight. She had been crying.

She had also been trying to dig into the forest floor with some odd kind of flat-headed spear, which had the glint of metal about it. That was stupid; it was all roots and rocks, and there was a very small heap of rocks next to her. There was something else, too, large and wrapped up. Perhaps I did walk in the footsteps of **Locaha**, Mau thought, because I know that there is a dead man in there. And the ghost girl, she was in my nightmares.

I am not alone.

The girl dropped the flat-headed spear and quickly held up something else, something that also shone like metal.

'I kn-know how to use this!' she shouted very loudly. 'One step more and I will pull the trigger, I mean it!' The metal thing waved back and forth in her hands. 'Don't think I'm afraid! I'm not afraid! I could have killed you before! Just because I felt sorry for you doesn't mean you can come down here! My father will be here soon!'

She sounded excited. Mau took the view that she wanted him to have the metal thing, because by the way she was holding it with both hands and waving it about she was obviously very frightened of it.

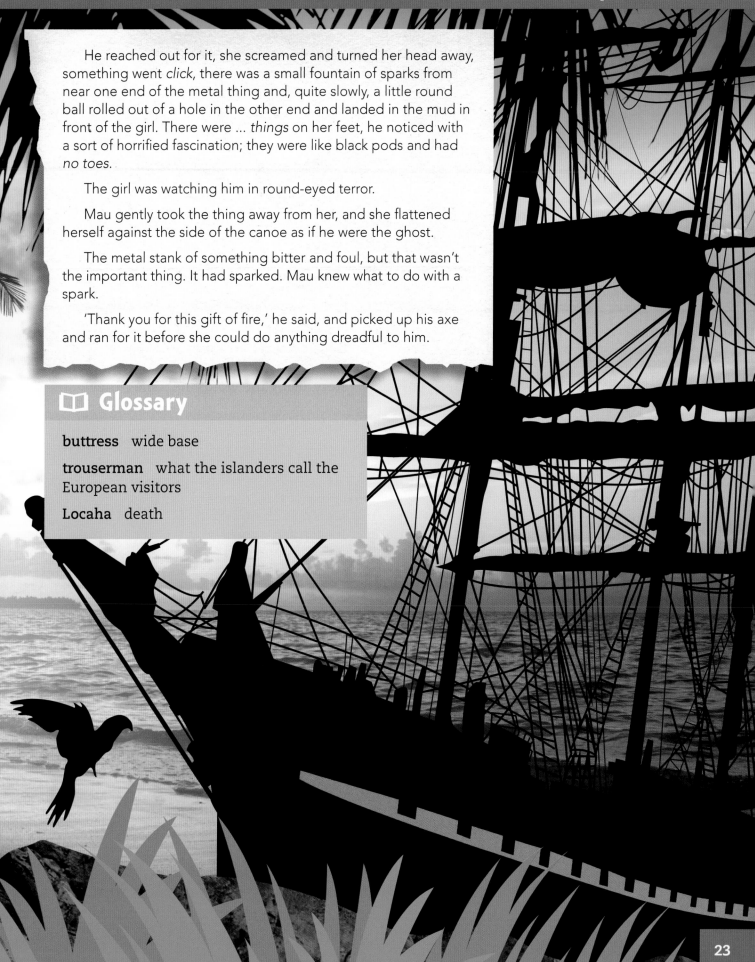

He reached out for it, she screamed and turned her head away, something went *click*, there was a small fountain of sparks from near one end of the metal thing and, quite slowly, a little round ball rolled out of a hole in the other end and landed in the mud in front of the girl. There were ... *things* on her feet, he noticed with a sort of horrified fascination; they were like black pods and had *no toes*.

The girl was watching him in round-eyed terror.

Mau gently took the thing away from her, and she flattened herself against the side of the canoe as if he were the ghost.

The metal stank of something bitter and foul, but that wasn't the important thing. It had sparked. Mau knew what to do with a spark.

'Thank you for this gift of fire,' he said, and picked up his axe and ran for it before she could do anything dreadful to him.

📖 Glossary

buttress wide base

trouserman what the islanders call the European visitors

Locaha death

6 Survival Skills

↺ Objective

Explore the effects of writing in the first person.

📖 Glossary

first-person narrative story or experience told using the words 'I' and 'we'

karabiner a metal ring used by rockclimbers to attach themselves safely to things

Dream the name of the climb

urbanity [in this context] living in a town or city

third-person narrative story or experience told by someone outside the story, using the words 'he', 'she', 'they'

Real-life adventurers can frequently find themselves in dangerous situations. Often this is conveyed through writing in the **first person**. The following extract is from an autobiography written by Heather Dawe, one of the UK's leading endurance athletes. In this extract, she describes an experience while climbing a sea cliff in North Wales with her friend Nirvana.

Extract from *Adventures in Mind* by Heather Dawe

The **karabiner** made a hollow 'plop' sound as it hit the water beneath us. A wave of realisation and vertigo suddenly washed over me. That sea is real. These cliffs are no place for me – what am I doing here? All it takes is one slip and it could be me hitting the water and quickly sinking as all of my climbing ironmongery drags me down. I felt exposed and, while she was a rope's length away from me, I knew Nirvana was uneasy too. I felt like I was losing control.

The trick with climbing in such places is to turn off the part of your brain that alerts you to the danger you should usually associate with that situation. If you climb enough, you become numbed to this alert, so accustomed to the exposure formed by height, space and location that it's normal. Right there, paused halfway up *Dream*, these places were very normal for me. Hanging around on high mountain crags and sea cliffs formed a regular part of my weekend escapes from **urbanity**. That a falling piece of climbing gear, dropped by my climbing partner, broke this state of mind for me was telling. The sound of the karabiner hitting the sea was all it took.

✎ Activities

1 How does the writer convey the danger of the situation? Using a table like the one below, select specific words and phrases and comment on how they add to the sense of danger.

Words/phrases conveying danger	Effect
'hit the water'	suggests height

2a Writing in the first person can make a significant difference to how a reader reacts to a text. Looking again at the extract, how does writing in the first person make you, the reader, feel?

2b What difference does it make to you as you read the text that you know that this experience really happened to the writer?

2c Imagine that the book had been a biography, therefore written in the **third person** (he/she). What difference would that make to your reaction to this extract?

SPAG

3 Write a piece for your school newspaper or magazine in which you describe, in the first person, a dangerous experience that happened to you (real or imagined). Aim to write around 200 words and try to sustain a sense of drama or danger throughout your piece. If possible, you might also like to include the second person (you).

↔ Stretch

Why does the writer switch to writing in the second person (you) in the second paragraph? What is the effect of this on the reader?

7 At the Extremes

↺ Objective

Compare diaries and blogs from different time periods.

Adventurers can face life at the extremes. Over a century ago, explorers raced to be the first to reach the South Pole, while today astronauts in space have opened a new frontier of exploration.

ignite INTERVIEW

'Whether you are climbing a mountain or writing a book, it's hard. But you have to keep going.'

Mick Conefrey

✎ Activities

1 Discuss the reasons why adventurers such as explorers and astronauts keep diaries or blogs. What can we learn from these as readers?

2a Read the extract from Captain Scott's diary on page 27. This describes the last days of the Antarctic explorer's failed expedition to be the first to reach the South Pole. Look at the opening paragraph. How does Scott's style of writing suggest that this is his personal journal?

2b Look at the second paragraph. What clues do you have that Scott isn't just writing the diary for himself?

2c What does Scott want readers of his diary to think about Captain Oates? Pick out details to support the points you make.

▤ Support

Think about:

- how Scott refers to Captain Oates
- how Scott describes Captain Oates's actions
- what Scott says about Captain Oates.

Extract from the journal of Captain Scott

Friday, March 16 or Saturday 17– Lost track of dates, but think the last correct. Tragedy all along the line. At lunch, the day before yesterday, poor Titus Oates said he couldn't go on; he proposed we should leave him in his sleeping-bag. That we could not do, and we induced him to come on, on the afternoon march. In spite of its awful nature for him he struggled on and we made a few miles. At night he was worse and we knew the end had come.

Should this be found I want these facts recorded. Oates' last thoughts were of his Mother, but immediately before he took pride in thinking that his regiment would be pleased with the bold way in which he met his death. We can testify to his bravery. He has **borne** intense suffering for weeks without complaint, and to the very last was able and willing to discuss outside subjects. He did not – would not – give up hope till the very end. He was a brave soul. This was the end. He slept through the night before last, hoping not to wake; but he woke in the morning – yesterday. It was blowing a blizzard. He said, 'I am just going outside and may be some time.' He went out into the blizzard and we have not seen him since.

📖 Glossary

borne   endured

adverbs   words which describe how an action is carried out, e.g. *happily, angrily*

Now read the extract from Luca Parmitano's blog on pages 28–29. Here, the astronaut describes the moment when his spacewalk, to carry out repairs outside the International Space Station, hits a problem.

3 How does Luca Parmitano build up tension in his description of his spacewalk? Discuss:

- the way he describes what happens and his actions
- the vocabulary he uses to share his thoughts and emotions
- his use of fronted adverbials and other organizational features.

Fronted adverbials are **adverbs** and adverbial phrases that are placed at the front of a sentence for emphasis. Fronted adverbials such as 'At this exact moment' and 'Finally' show the sequence of time in this piece of writing.

SPAG

4 You have been asked to select one of these two texts for a school display about real-life adventurers. Write an email to the school council explaining which text you would choose and why.

More to explore

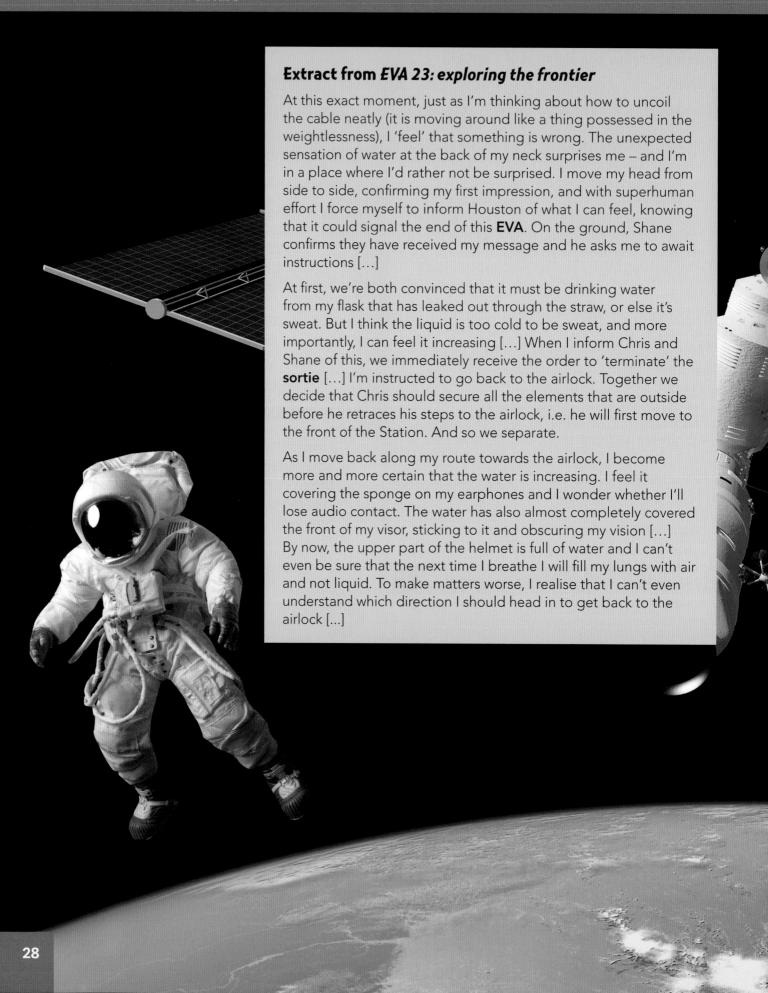

Extract from *EVA 23: exploring the frontier*

At this exact moment, just as I'm thinking about how to uncoil the cable neatly (it is moving around like a thing possessed in the weightlessness), I 'feel' that something is wrong. The unexpected sensation of water at the back of my neck surprises me – and I'm in a place where I'd rather not be surprised. I move my head from side to side, confirming my first impression, and with superhuman effort I force myself to inform Houston of what I can feel, knowing that it could signal the end of this **EVA**. On the ground, Shane confirms they have received my message and he asks me to await instructions [...]

At first, we're both convinced that it must be drinking water from my flask that has leaked out through the straw, or else it's sweat. But I think the liquid is too cold to be sweat, and more importantly, I can feel it increasing [...] When I inform Chris and Shane of this, we immediately receive the order to 'terminate' the **sortie** [...] I'm instructed to go back to the airlock. Together we decide that Chris should secure all the elements that are outside before he retraces his steps to the airlock, i.e. he will first move to the front of the Station. And so we separate.

As I move back along my route towards the airlock, I become more and more certain that the water is increasing. I feel it covering the sponge on my earphones and I wonder whether I'll lose audio contact. The water has also almost completely covered the front of my visor, sticking to it and obscuring my vision [...] By now, the upper part of the helmet is full of water and I can't even be sure that the next time I breathe I will fill my lungs with air and not liquid. To make matters worse, I realise that I can't even understand which direction I should head in to get back to the airlock [...]

I try to contact Chris and Shane. I listen as they talk to each other, but their voices are very faint now. I can hardly hear them and they can't hear me. I'm alone. I frantically think of a plan [...] It's not much, but it's the best idea I have: to follow the cable to the airlock [...]

Finally, with a huge sense of relief, I peer through the curtain of water before my eyes and make out the thermal cover of the airlock: just a little further and I'll be safe [...] Moving with my eyes closed, I manage to get inside and position myself to wait for Chris' return. I sense movement behind me; Chris enters the airlock and judging from the vibrations, I know that he's closing the hatch [...]

Now that we are repressurizing, I know that if the water does overwhelm me I can always open the helmet. I'll probably lose consciousness, but in any case that would be better than drowning inside the helmet.

 Glossary

EVA extra-vehicular activity, e.g. a spacewalk

sortie mission

⏱ Extra Time

1. What do both extracts suggest about team spirit and how is this expressed?

2. Write your own blog or diary entry about an adventure you have had or would like to have.

8 Worth the Risk?

↺ Objective

Discuss whether dangerous pursuits have any place in the modern world.

Nowadays, you don't need to be an adventurer to take part in dangerous pursuits. Adventure holidays and extreme sports give ordinary people the chance to find the thrills that explorers and other intrepid adventurers faced in the past. But are these activities worth the risk?

✎ Activities

1 Read Simon Jenkins' opinion column on page 31. Summarize what his views are on why people travel overseas to take part in extreme sports and dangerous activities.

2 What examples does Simon Jenkins give to support his point of view? Do you find these persuasive?

3 Your school has asked the student council to discuss a proposal to include adventure sports and activities such as climbing, kayaking and BMX biking in the P.E. curriculum. Follow the steps on the right to discuss this proposal and agree on a decision.

Preparation: Note down your own thoughts and ideas on this proposal. Identify the most relevant points and place these in order of importance. Add explanations and examples to the ideas you think you will use in the discussion.

Discussion: Share your ideas. Listen to others and build on their ideas to move the discussion forward. Ask **open questions** to encourage others to explain or expand their contributions.

Decision: Summarize the points of view for and against the proposal. Vote to reach a decision on the proposal. Prepare a brief explanation of your decision and the reasons for it.

FROM GREENLAND TO MOUNT EVEREST, THIS IS THE SEASON OF RECKLESS JAUNTS

A young Briton dies trying to cross Greenland in a blizzard. Another goes missing while trying to sail the Pacific. Three climbers narrowly escape death in a mob fight on Mount Everest. Three sailors plan to pedalo across the Atlantic. That is all inside a week…

This is the season when crazy tourism **goes viral**, when "gappers" dream up dangerous adventures and when no holiday is complete without some display of **machismo**. The latest to boom are base jumping, hang-gliding, cave-diving and cycling across deserts.

We once thought this was merely a British craving to escape the Health and Safety Executive. If boys can no longer dive into a local swimming pool, they will dive off a Greek cliff. If they are not allowed to ride a horse without a crash helmet and sack of insurance certificates, they will ride a bull in Pamplona. Take adventure out of Britain and you take Britain out of adventure…

Back in time, taking risk was life and death. Miners, sailors, builders, quarrymen suffered appalling injuries to support their families. To early explorers danger was the price of discovery. Columbus would not have set sail in a pedalo. Edmund Hillary would not have climbed Everest without oxygen. Risking death as a pastime would have seemed irrational, except for sports with origins in military prowess, such as hunting, boxing and fencing.

The mad and mostly illegal sport of base jumping – from a cliff with a parachute – now sees some 15 deaths a year. One jump in 60 is said to end in a fatality and a successful jump is "one you survive". A high risk of death or injury attends pursuits such as motorbiking, big-wave surfing, altitude climbing and, a new craze, **street luging**. People even go sailing off the Somalian coast to defy the pirates.

All these people are seeking thrills which, by definition, they cannot find at home. Home nowadays is beyond tame. School pupils cannot swim in Snowdonia lakes without trained lifesavers on hand. Children cannot go kayaking without attendant motor boats. You need a safety course to go on a hill walk.

📖 Glossary

open question   a question which cannot be simply answered by 'yes' or 'no'

goes viral   spreads rapidly

machismo   an exaggerated sense of manliness

street luging   riding a sledge down a steep road

9 Assessment: Analysing Literary Non-fiction Extracts

Your Head Teacher is delivering an assembly to a local Primary school about the adventure of moving to Secondary school. She wants to begin her assembly with a reading about explorers who have been brave enough to break new ground. She has asked Year 7 students to choose which of the following two extracts she should read and to explain why this extract will appeal to Year 6 students.

The first is an extract from *The Lost City of Z* by David Grann, which describes the British explorer Colonel Percy Harrison Fawcett's expedition party coming under attack in the Amazon jungle. The second extract is written by the explorer Kira Salak and describes her encounter with a witch doctor in Papua New Guinea.

Having read both extracts, choose one to analyse. Use the skills you have developed throughout this unit to write a letter to your Head Teacher explaining why your chosen extract will hold the attention of the Year 6 audience. In your letter you should refer to evidence from the extract and comment on:

- the situation the explorer finds themselves in and how they react

- what the extract suggests about the dangers involved in exploration

- the devices which the writer uses to make the passage exciting, such as sentence structure, vocabulary, imagery and dialogue.

Planning your letter…

Read both extracts and select the one you want to analyse. Think about the bullet points on the left as you re-read the extract. Make notes of any details that you think it might be helpful to refer to when you write your letter to the Head Teacher.

Writing your letter…

Remember that in your letter, you will need to:

- Use **Standard English**.

- Refer to evidence and quotations from the text.

- Start with an introductory paragraph.

- Group your analysis of the extract into separate paragraphs.

- Finish with a clear conclusion.

Note that, for the purposes of this assessment, you will be marked on your reading and analysis skills, rather than on your writing skills.

Extract from *The Lost City of Z* by David Grann

A member of Fawcett's team dived into the water, shouting, "Retire! Retire!" But Fawcett insisted on pulling the boats to the opposite bank, as arrows continued to cascade from the sky. "One of these came within a foot of my head, and I actually saw the face of the savage who fired it," Costin later recalled. Fawcett ordered his men to drop their rifles, but the barrage of arrows persisted. And so Fawcett instructed one of the men, as further demonstration of their peaceful intentions, to pull out his accordion and play it. The rest of the party, commanded to stand and face their deaths without protest, sang along as Costin, first in a trembling voice, then more fervently, called out the words to "The Soldiers of the Queen": "In the fight for England's glory, lads / Of its world wide glory let us sing."

Fawcett then did something that shocked Costin so much that he would recall it vividly even as an old man: the major untied the handkerchief around his neck and, waving it above his head, waded into the river, heading directly into the **fusillade** of arrows. Over the years, Fawcett had picked up scraps of Indian dialects, scribbling the words in his logbooks and studying them at night, and he called out the few fragments of vocabulary he knew, repeating friend, friend, friend, not sure if the word that he was shouting was even right, as the water from the river rose to his armpits. Then the arrows ceased. For a moment, no one moved as Fawcett stood in the river, hands above head, like a **penitent** being baptized. According to Costin, an Indian appeared from behind a tree and came down to the edge of the river. Paddling out towards Fawcett in a raft, he took the handkerchief from Fawcett's hand. "The Major made signs for him to be taken across," Costin later recounted in a letter to his daughter, and the Indian "poled back to his side with Fawcett kneeling on his flimsy craft."

"On climbing the opposite bank," Fawcett said, "I had the unpleasant anticipation of receiving a shot in the face or an arrow in the stomach."

The Indians led him away. "[Fawcett] disappeared into the forest, and we were left wondering!" Costin said. The party feared that its leader had been slaughtered until, nearly an hour later, he emerged from the jungle with an Indian cheerfully wearing his Stetson.

📖 Glossary

Standard English   the variety of English that is regarded as 'correct' and is used in more formal situations. It is not specific to any geographical area and can be spoken or written.

fusillade   a series of shots in quick succession

penitent   someone repenting for their sins

Extract from *Four Corners: A Journey into the Heart of Papua New Guinea* by Kira Salak

It's the late afternoon when we leave the canoe behind for a hike to the witch doctor's village. We follow a faint, muddy path through **primeval** jungle, trees towering at least a hundred feet above us, vines creeping from limb to limb, hugging trunks and hanging from boughs like gigantic tentacles.

The path opens up. We see a small village on the edge of a large stream. Mountains of rain forest rise to the south, clouds **languishing** about them, the departing sun already warming the sky and jungle with an orange glow. Everything looks softened, as if a god were resting a gentle hand upon the earth, quieting it, preparing it for rest. Joseph calls out. Some kids playing in a stream look at us, freeze, then run off in terror.

"They never see white people," Joseph explains.

A man in a dingy, unbuttoned white shirt, wearing a breechcloth and **pandanus** leaves around his waist, comes out to greet us. **Cassowary** claws erupt from the tops of each of his nostrils, and large hoop earrings made from bird **quills** graze his shoulders. A band of bright red and yellow beads encircles his head.

"This is the Chief," Joseph says. "The witch doctor."

The Chief looks at us sternly before he disappears into the jungle. Confused, we soon hear a low-pitched, ominous whooping coming from nearby. Suddenly a man bursts forth with spear held aloft. Bright yellow paint covers his body. Pandanus leaves are tied about his arms and legs. He charges toward us with a sharp holler, and I find myself running for my life. I retreat toward the village but am quickly cut off, the Chief's spear only inches from my face.

He smiles. I try to smile back. Thirty years ago, I may have actually been speared. Now he lowers the spear and shows it to me. He insists I run my fingers down the length of its shaft, touch the sharp bamboo point. Jens comes over, and thus begins a heated discussion about whether the spear is for sale and how much it costs. Rob wants a spear, too, and so the Chief's friend runs off to his hut to get some more. It's the Home Shopping Network, **PNG-style**, spears, bows and arrows laid out for our **kina**. Jens pulls off his T-shirt and exchanges it for several arrows.

I wander off along the stream, watching the mountains growing increasingly pink in the declining light. Children hide behind the posts of the stilt huts, watching me silently. An old woman wearing only a grass skirt comes toward me and hands me a few of the mourning necklaces she's made. She pats my hand, says something to me, and smiles a toothless grin. Thinking she's trying to sell them to me, I reach for some kina to pay her, but she shakes her head and speaks softly to me in her **tok ples** language. She pats my hand again and I watch her shuffle off, back bent, bare feet following the ground's well-worn path. I am beginning to understand.

📖 Glossary

primeval   ancient

languishing   growing weak

pandanus   a tropical tree

cassowary   a large flightless bird from Papua New Guinea

quills   bird feathers

PNG-style   Papua New Guinea style

kina   money used in Papua New Guinea

tok ples   language used by the tribes in Papua New Guinea

2

The Identity Kit

Who am I?

Introduction

Your identity is what makes you *you* – a unique individual.

The question 'Who am I?' is important from when we are first given a name: through getting to know our family and friends to going to school, getting a job and enjoying our hobbies. Everyone wonders about their identity. Some people write about it: in poems, songs, plays, novels and even autobiographies, all trying to answer the question 'Who am I?'

This unit will give you the opportunity to enjoy reading and listening to some of these texts, and to write some of your own. You will develop your skills as an analyst and wordsmith.

ignite INTERVIEW
Dreadlock Alien, Performance poet

A new poem starts with the words gathered around a subject. I like poems that challenge concepts. Writing is an individual task; you write about what you know and those experiences build up your identity. Poetry is a good way to write about yourself and your past but also a good way to find out about other people's cultures. I am a performance poet. A performance poet connects directly with the audience: it's live and immediate every time you perform a poem.

✎ Activities

1a Write one short sentence about your life, e.g. '**The cat ran away this morning**' or '**My room was a mess when I left it.**'

1b Exchange your sentence with a partner. Using a thesaurus or dictionary, elaborate on and improve your partner's sentence, e.g. '**The excitable cat trotted off into the misty dawn**' or '**My private den was a chaotic heap as I flew from the house.**'

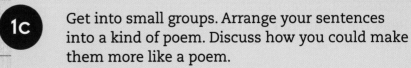

1c Get into small groups. Arrange your sentences into a kind of poem. Discuss how you could make them more like a poem.

1 What's in a Name?

↻ Objectives

- Explore the use of imagery and rhetorical features in conveying meaning.

- Establish a viewpoint in non-fiction writing.

Our names are our labels. They identify us as individuals. Before we are born, our families think long and hard about what to call us, knowing that our names will mean something to them, to us and to everyone else we meet throughout our life.

✎ Activities

1 Think about your own name.
- Do you like it? (Explain why or why not.)
- Does it have a special meaning?
- If you could choose your own name, what would it be and why?

In the poem on the right, a poet expresses his feelings about his name. Read the poem and then complete Activities 2–4.

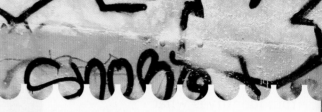

'Isn't My Name Magical?' by James Berry

Nobody can see my name on me.
My name is inside
and all over me, unseen
like other people also keep it.
Isn't my name magic?

My name is mine only.
It tells I am individual,
the one special person it shakes
when I'm wanted.

If I'm with hundreds of people
and my name gets called,
my sound switches me on to answer
like it was my human electricity.
Isn't that magical?

My name echoes across playground,
it comes, it demands my attention.
I have to find out who calls,
who wants me for what.
My name gets blurted out in class,
it is a terror, at a bad time,
because somebody is cross.

My name gets called in a whisper
I am happy, because
my name may have touched me
with a loving voice.
Isn't it all magic?

2 What is your initial reaction to this poem? The poet describes his name as 'magical'. What do you think he means by this?

3 What image do these lines create in the reader's mind: 'My name is inside / and all over me, unseen'?

4 The poet repeats a similar question in different verses. Why do you think he does this? What effect does it have on the reader?

Tagging is a form of vandalism.

Tagging is an art form which expresses people's sense of identity.

We often label things with our names to identify them as ours. For some people, like Ashley in the extract below, this goes beyond just labelling our possessions.

Tightrope
by Gillian Cross

[...] her concentration sharpened and she focused on the wall. Steadily she walked along the ridge towards it [...]

She knew exactly what she was going to do. No fancy pictures. Those were fine in the right place – she had a brilliant Mickey Mouse on the side of Nightingale House – but this was the sort of wall where you had to write your tag or nothing. And she was going to do it full size in four colours. With shadows, to show she'd taken her time.

She pulled out the black can and stood there, feeling the adrenalin come. It would only take one wrong line to blow the whole thing – but she wasn't going to blow it.

Her finger pushed down on the button.

She laid out the letters as if they were dancing.

5 What do you think the 'tag' is?

6 Choose one of the views in the speech bubbles on the left and write a short letter to your local paper about 'tagging' in your town.

◈ Support

You could start your letter:

Dear Editor,

Walking through the town yesterday, I was surprised to see...

ignite INTERVIEW

'My real name is Mr Grant, but I write and perform under the name Dreadlock Alien.'

Dreadlock Alien

2 Childhood Revisited

↺ Objective

Revisit childhood stories and poems, exploring the effects of rhyme and rhythm.

From when we are babies and toddlers, we start to learn about the world around us and our place in it. Some of this learning comes through nursery rhymes, stories and poems, which have often been handed down from generation to generation. They often warn children of dangers, give them models of good behaviour and remind them of things that have happened.

✎ Activities

1 With a partner, try to remember some nursery rhymes. Talk about what they might mean, or what message they might carry. For example, 'Ring a Ring o' Roses' warned people about the symptoms of the plague.

Rhyme and **rhythm** have always been popular in children's poems, partly because they helped early storytellers to remember them, but also because patterns of language are soothing and reassuring to young children, and they can be fun. They also contribute to our experience of learning to read.

Read the extract from *The Gruffalo*. The mouse in the story tricks other animals in the woods into leaving him alone by pretending to be friends with the Gruffalo. Then, of course, he meets the real Gruffalo.

Extract from *The Gruffalo* by Julia Donaldson

But who is this creature with terrible claws

And terrible teeth in his terrible jaws?

He has knobbly knees and turned-out toes

And a poisonous wart at the end of his nose.

His eyes are orange, his tongue is black;

He has purple prickles all over his back.

"Oh help! Oh no!

It's a gruffalo!"

"My favourite food!" the Gruffalo said.

"You'll taste good on a slice of bread!"

"Good?" said the mouse. "Don't call me good!

I'm the scariest creature in this wood.

Just walk behind me and soon you'll see,

Everyone is afraid of me."

"All right," said the Gruffalo, bursting with laughter.

"You go ahead and I'll follow after."

After this, they meet the snake and the owl. Both are frightened away from the mouse by the presence of the Gruffalo behind him.

2 What do you think is the message of this story? Explain your answer carefully, choosing parts of the text to show what you mean.

3 Think about the character of the mouse. What qualities does he have that help him to survive?

4 List some of the features of this poem that you think would appeal to younger children.

5 Count the number of **syllables** in each line. What do you notice? Does this make a difference to the rhythm of the piece?

6 This poem is written in **rhyming couplets**. Explain what this means in your own words, using examples from the text.

📖 Glossary

rhyme words which have the same final sound, e.g. 'treat', 'meet'

rhythm a regularly repeated beat

syllable a word or part of a word that has one vowel sound when you say it, e.g. 'cat' has one syllable, 'din-o-saur' has three syllables

rhyming couplets two lines of a similar length, next to each other, that rhyme

🕐 Extra Time

Rewrite the verse as a short piece of prose, avoiding any rhyming words and using sentences instead of lines. Then read the two different versions aloud. What difference do the rhythm and the rhyme make? Which do you prefer and why?

③ Who We Would Like to Be

↺ Objectives

Investigate how patterns of language can help to convey a theme.

Some writers have used poetry to give readers an identity to aspire to. In 1895 Rudyard Kipling wrote the poem 'If...'. It was inspired by a British soldier, who Kipling believed showed all the qualities that people should strive to have.

Read the poem carefully. It is narrated (spoken) by a father, talking to his son. The father is advising his son that if he can behave in a certain way, he will mature into a 'real man'.

'If...' by Rudyard Kipling

If you can keep your head when all about you
Are losing theirs and blaming it on you,
If you can trust yourself when all men doubt you,
But make allowance for their doubting too;
If you can wait and not be tired by waiting,
Or being lied about, don't deal in lies,
Or being hated, don't give way to hating,
And yet don't look too good, nor talk too wise:

If you can dream – and not make dreams your master;
If you can think – and not make thoughts your aim;
If you can meet with Triumph and Disaster
And treat those two impostors just the same;
If you can bear to hear the truth you've spoken
Twisted by knaves to make a trap for fools,
Or watch the things you gave your life to, broken,
And stoop and build 'em up with worn-out tools:

If you can make one heap of all your winnings
And risk it on one turn of pitch-and-toss,
And lose, and start again at your beginnings
And never breathe a word about your loss;
If you can force your heart and nerve and sinew
To serve your turn long after they are gone,
And so hold on when there is nothing in you
Except the Will which says to them: "Hold on!"

If you can talk with crowds and keep your virtue,
Or walk with Kings – nor lose the common touch,
If neither foes nor loving friends can hurt you,
If all men count with you, but none too much;
If you can fill the unforgiving minute
With sixty seconds' worth of distance run,
Yours is the Earth and everything that's in it,
And – which is more – you'll be a man, my son!

✏ Activities

1 The narrator is giving his son lots of examples of how to behave. Read the advice in the speech bubbles on the right. Each one is a simpler version of some of the advice given in the poem. Match each one to the original lines in the first verse.

2 Look at the **rhyme scheme** of the poem. Jot down the pattern of rhymes, using the letters A, B, C, D.

↔ Stretch

Why are the first four lines of the rhyme scheme different?

3 Many words and phrases are repeated in the poem. Pick them out and talk about the effect. Does it make the message stronger?

4 Make up a one-verse poem of your own, using the same structure as 'If…'.

- Decide who your narrator will be and to whom they are talking.
- Think of the overall aim for the last line first.
- Think of some advice to give.

📖 Glossary

rhyme scheme pattern of rhyming lines in a poem. We use letters of the alphabet like a code to show rhyming patterns. The first two lines that rhyme we label 'A', the next two 'B', and so on. Note that the rhyming lines don't necessarily follow each other.

Don't hate people, even if they seem to hate you.

Don't dress to show off or talk just to impress people.

Keep calm, even when everyone else panics.

4 How Other People See Us

↺ Objective

Understand how a narrative viewpoint contributes to a text.

 Activities

SPAG

1 Write down three **adjectives** that you think describe yourself (your character, not your looks). Then write down three adjectives that you would use to describe your partner. Share your descriptions with your partner. Talk about whether you see yourself the same way other people see you.

As we grow up, we become more aware of our individual identity and also more aware of how other people see us. There is often a difference between how we see ourselves, how other people see us and how we want to be seen.

In the novel *Wonder*, the author R. J. Palacio explores the confusion of identity that a young boy feels as he grows up and tries to fit in at a new school. Read the extract on the right and then complete Activities 2–5.

Extract from *Wonder* by R. J. Palacio

I know I'm not an ordinary ten-year-old kid. I mean, sure, I do ordinary things. I eat ice cream. I ride my bike. I play ball. I have an Xbox. Stuff like that makes me ordinary. I guess. And I feel ordinary. Inside. But I know ordinary kids don't make other ordinary kids run away screaming in playgrounds. I know ordinary kids don't get stared at wherever they go.

If I found a magic lamp and I could have one wish, I would wish that I had a normal face that no one ever noticed at all. I would wish that I could walk down the street without people seeing me and then doing that look-away thing [...]

But I'm kind of used to how I look by now. I know how to pretend I don't see the faces people make. We've all gotten pretty good at that sort of thing: me, Mom and Dad, Via. Actually, I take that back: Via's not so good at it. She can get really annoyed when people do something rude. Like, for instance, one time in the playground some older kids made some noises [...] she just started yelling at the kids [...].

Via doesn't see me as ordinary. She says she does, but if I were ordinary, she wouldn't feel like she needs to protect me as much. And Mom and Dad don't see me as ordinary either. They see me as extraordinary. I think the only person in the world who realizes how ordinary I am is me.

2   What do you learn about the narrator (the character who is telling the story) in this extract? Write down at least two things about his personality and one thing about his looks.

3   How does his sense of identity differ from how other people see him?

4   Why do you think the writer chose to write this story as a **first-person narrative**? What effect does this have? Do you think it would be as powerful if it were written as a **third-person narrative**?

SPAG

5   Look carefully at the language in the extract. What effect does it have on how the reader feels about the character?

☑ Progress Check

Write another short paragraph to add to the extract. Try to use the same narrative voice and language style as the original.

Swap your work with a partner. Ask them to assess you on a scale of 1 to 3 (3 being the highest) on how well you:

- kept using the first-person narrative voice (e.g. the **pronouns** 'I', 'me', 'we')

- used the same **colloquial** informal style

- included some American English.

📖 Glossary

adjective   word that describes a noun, e.g. *happy*, *blue*, *furious*

first-person narrative   story told by a character, using the words 'I' and 'we'

third-person narrative   story told by someone outside the story, using the words 'he', 'she', 'they'

pronoun   a word used instead of a noun

colloquial   suitable for conversation rather than formal speech or writing

5 How Other People Judge Us

↻ Objective

Use inference to recognize the deeper meaning of a text.

Sometimes a poem has more than one layer of meaning. There is the surface, obvious meaning, but underneath, the reader has to **infer** what the deeper message of the poem is.

Read the poem on this page, thinking carefully about what the author describes and what the deeper meaning might be. (There is a clue in the title.)

📖 Glossary

infer work something out from what is said or done, even though it is not actually said directly

personification giving an object human qualities

intonation the rise and fall of a person's voice when they speak

'Differences'
by Sophie Hannah

Not everyone who wears a hat
Is copying the Queen.
Not everything that's large and flat
Thinks it's a movie screen.
If every time I dress in blue
I imitate the sea,
It makes no difference what I do –
Nothing is down to me.

Not every dim, electric light
Would like to be the sun.
A water pistol doesn't quite
Mimic a loaded gun.
I do my best, I do my worst
With my specific heart –
God and the Devil got there first;
They had an early start.

Tomatoes can be round and red
Yet be distinct from Mars.
Not all the things above my head
Can be described as stars.

The world had better learn what's what
(If it remotely cares) –
A ladder is a ladder, not
A failed attempt at stairs.

Activities

1 Think about times when you feel you have been criticized or judged unfairly, for example by your parents, friends or a teacher. Describe how it made you feel.

2 In the poem, the poet gives us examples of unfair comparisons. Pick out three and explain why the comparisons are unfair. For example: 'In the first verse, the poem is saying that people who wear hats might wear them for lots of different reasons. It doesn't mean that they want to be like the Queen, who always wears a hat at formal public events.'

3 The poet uses **personification** to mirror the idea of people being judged as something they are not. What human qualities are being attributed to non-living things? Why do you think the poet does this?

4 What can you infer about the main message of the poem? Write a short introduction to the poem for a poetry website, giving your interpretation of:

- who it may have been written for (audience)
- why it may have been written (purpose).

Use evidence from the text to support your inferences.

5 Brackets and dashes are a form of punctuation that help readers' understanding.

They can be used:

- to show a break in a sentence that is longer or more important than a comma
- to add an explanation
- to show an interruption or an afterthought.

Look at where the poet uses brackets and dashes in the poem. Explain why they are used and what effect they have.

SPAG

6 The punctuation in the poem also gives clues as to how it might be spoken if read aloud.

Prepare to recite this whole poem aloud, thinking carefully about pace, volume, pauses, **intonation** and any actions you might add to give impact.

6 Collective Identity

↺ Objective

Explore how language features associated with one text type can be used creatively in another.

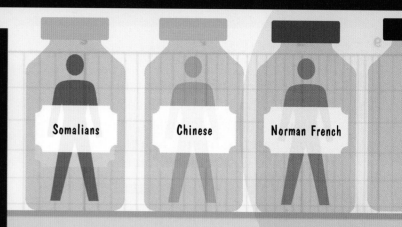

As well as our own individual identity, most people feel they have a group identity, too. This might be feeling like a part of a wider family, a team, a religion, a community or a nation, or a mix of these.

In his poem 'The British', Benjamin Zephaniah looks at many of the different racial influences that have contributed over time to create the rich multi-layered identity the British nation has today.

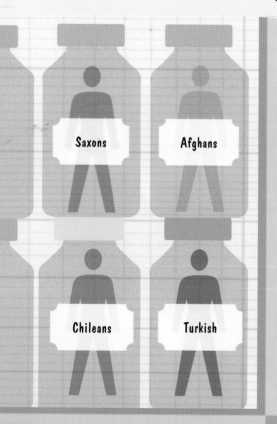

✎ Activities

1 Look at the structure of this poem. What type of non-fiction text does it remind you of and why?

▨ Support

Look at the commands and the step-by-step approach. Also, think about words such as 'simmer'.

2 What **extended metaphor** is the poet using to convey the history of the British nation? Identify some words and phrases that help to build up the **metaphor** and note your ideas in a spider diagram.

3 Explain why the poet's metaphor is a good one to describe the identity of the British people.

4 What does the poet suggest about the English language? How important does he feel it is for the nation's identity?

'The British'
by Benjamin Zephaniah

Take some Picts, Celts and Silures
And let them settle,
Then overrun them with Roman conquerors.

Remove the Romans after approximately 400 years
Add lots of Norman French to some
Angles, Saxons, Jutes and Vikings, then stir vigorously.

Mix some hot Chileans, cool Jamaicans, Dominicans,
Trinidadians and Bajans with some Ethiopians, Chinese,
Vietnamese and Sudanese.

Then take a blend of Somalians, Sri Lankans, Nigerians
And Pakistanis,
Combine with some Guyanese
And turn up the heat.

Sprinkle some fresh Indians, Malaysians, Bosnians,
Iraqis and Bangladeshis together with some
Afghans, Spanish, Turkish, Kurdish, Japanese
And Palestinians
Then add to the melting pot.

Leave the ingredients to simmer.

As they mix and blend allow their languages to flourish
Binding them together with English.

Allow time to be cool.

Add some unity, understanding, and respect for the future,
Serve with justice
And enjoy.

Note: All the ingredients are equally important.
Treating one ingredient better than another will leave
a bitter unpleasant taste.
Warning: An unequal spread of justice will damage the
people and cause pain. Give justice and equality to all.

5 In pairs or small groups, create your own identity poem using an original extended metaphor if you can.

ignite INTERVIEW

'Whatever you know about, it is all part of your identity. So start with that. Write about something you know.'

Dreadlock Alien

📖 Glossary

metaphor describing something as something else, not meant to be taken literally, e.g. *You are a star.*

extended metaphor continuing the use of the metaphor throughout the whole text or a number of lines

7 Describing Other People

↺ Objective

Analyse the effects of imagery in characterization (describing characters).

When we describe real people or fictional characters, we try to make their identity as clear as possible. We often use imagery to conjure up pictures in the reader's mind. These images tell us something specific about the character, often in a memorable or amusing way.

✎ Activities

1 People often use literary devices, such as **similes**, to describe each other, for example, 'He's as quiet as a mouse'. Think of another common simile that is often used to describe people.

↔ Stretch

Write two new similes to describe a member of your family. Try to make them as imaginative as possible!

2a Think of one of your favourite characters from a book or film and describe him or her using a metaphor. For example: 'Gandalf is a tower of strength'.

2b Explain why you chose that image to describe your character. For example: 'A tower of strength makes Gandalf sound very powerful and strong. It creates an image in the reader's mind of something made out of stone, built to last and taller than the things around.'

📖 Glossary

simile a comparison that uses the words 'like' or 'as… as', e.g. *as white as snow*

Read the two texts A and B, noticing how they build up the identity of the characters with great vividness, using imagery and carefully chosen vocabulary.

A ### Extract from *The Outing: A Story* by Dylan Thomas

The extract is taken from a short story in which a young Welsh boy is taken on a day trip with his larger-than-life uncle. Here he describes his uncle and aunt.

I was staying at the time with my uncle and his wife. Although she was my aunt, I never thought of her as anything other than the wife of my uncle, partly because he was so big and trumpeting and red-hairy and used to fill every inch of the hot little house like an old buffalo squeezed into an airing cupboard, and partly because she was so small and silk and quick and made no noise at all as she whisked about on padded paws, dusting the china dogs, feeding the buffalo, setting the mousetraps that never caught her; and once she sleaked out of the room, to squeak in a nook or nibble in the hayloft, you forgot she had ever been there.

B ### Extract from *The Tall Woman and Her Short Husband* by Feng Ji-Cai

This extract is taken from a short story by a Chinese author. Here he describes the couple who give the story its title.

She seemed dried up and scrawny with a face like an unvarnished ping-pong bat. Her features would pass but they were small and insignificant as if carved in shallow relief. She was flat-chested, had a ramrod back and buttocks as scraggy as a scrubbing board. Her husband on the other hand seemed a rubber roly-poly: well-fleshed, solid and radiant. Everything about him – his calves, insteps, lips, nose and fingers – were like pudgy little meatballs […] His eyes were like two high-voltage light-bulbs, while his wife's were like glazed marbles. The two of them just did not match, and formed a marked contrast. But they were inseparable.

3 Choose the extract that you feel is most successful in creating a sense of the character's identity. Explain why the images that the author chooses in the text are so effective.

☑ Progress Check

Write a short character description of a couple in a new fiction text, using imagery. Ask a partner to comment on two strong aspects of your description and one aspect that could do with more thought.

8 Family and Identity

↻ Objective

Analyse how poets use layout and form to present their viewpoint.

Our sense of identity changes as we grow up, but it always has some links with our parents, or the people who cared for us as children. As adults, often with children of our own, our sense of who we are and who our parents are becomes clearer.

The following poems (below and on page 54) explore the relationship between parents and their children from different viewpoints. The poets use very different forms and structures to do this.

'Birth'
by Elise Paschen

Armored in red, her voice commands

every corner. Bells gong on squares,

in steeples, answering the prayers.

Bright tulips crown the **boulevards**.

Pulled from the womb she imitates

that **mythic** kick from some god's head.

She roars, and we are conquered.

Her legs, set free, combat the air.

Naked warrior: she is our own.

Entire empires are overthrown.

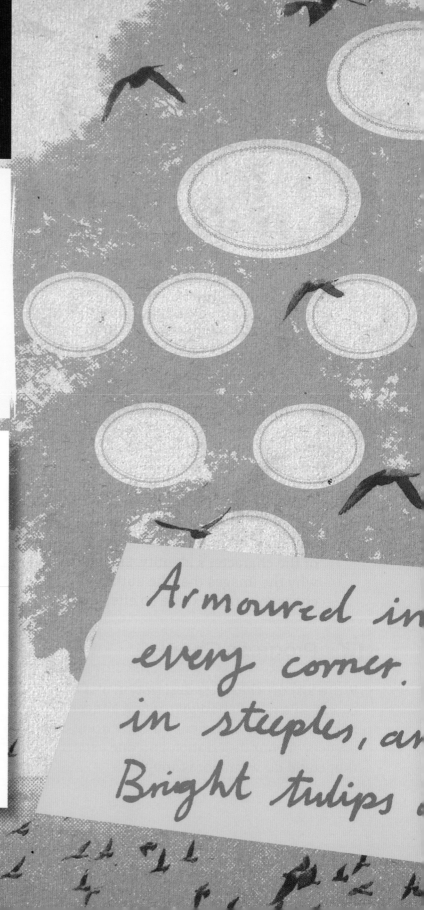

✏️ Activities

1a Who are the 'we' in the second verse of 'Birth'? Who is 'she'?

1b What two images contribute to the sense of celebration in the first verse?

1c Identify the combat imagery and explain what it suggests about the parents' attitude towards their daughter.

📖 Glossary

boulevard   a wide street, often with trees

mythic   from a myth (an ancient, traditional story)

2a Look at the form and layout of 'Birth'. Answer the questions below to explore their effect.

How does the rhythm of the poem change? (Look at the number of syllables in each line.) What effect does this slight change of rhythm have?

Jot down the number of lines in each verse. What is the effect of having a shorter final verse?

2b How else is the final couplet different from the lines in the previous verses? (Think about a popular poetic convention.)

ed, her voice commands
lls gong on squares
vering prayers
n the boulevards

More to
explore

Now read the second poem.

'Poem at Thirty-Nine' by Alice Walker

How I miss my father.
I wish he had not been
so tired
when I was born.

Writing deposit slips and checks
I think of him.
He taught me how.
This is the form,
he must have said:
the way it is done. I learned to see
bits of paper
as a way
to escape the life he knew
and even in high school
had a savings
account.

He taught me
that telling the truth
did not always mean
a beating;
though many of my truths
must have grieved him
before the end.

How I miss my father!
He cooked like a person
dancing
in a yoga meditation
and craved the voluptuous
sharing
of good food.

Now I look and cook just like him:
my brain light;
tossing this and that
into the pot;
seasoning none of my life
the same way twice; happy to feed
whoever strays my way.

He would have grown
to admire
the woman I've become:
cooking, writing, chopping wood,
staring into the fire.

📖 Glossary

free verse   poetry that has no regular form, rhyme scheme or rhythm

✏ Activities continued

3a 'Poem at Thirty-Nine' is written in **free verse**.

What is the impact of the single words on a line?

3b Which short line means the most to you? Explain why.

3c Why has the poet placed the stanza breaks where she has?

4 Which words or phrases do you think say the most about the father? Explain why.

5 This poem uses the speaker's age as its title. Decide on a new title that you think sums up the main message of the poet. Explain why.

▧ Support

You could choose one of the lines from the poem as the title, but you need to explain why you have chosen it.

↔ Stretch

Write a description of the person who is writing 'Poem at Thirty-Nine'.

🕐 Extra Time

Do you think the speaker of each poem is the poet themselves? Support your answer with evidence from the poems.

9 Respect and Influence

↺ Objectives

Explore how poetic devices and wordplay are used in a performance poem.

We all need to feel respected and valued. This reinforces a positive sense of our identity. Often we can choose to make others feel good about themselves, by showing respect and appreciation.

ignite INTERVIEW

'A live literature poet will maybe script in a pause or a gesture.'

Dreadlock Alien

✎ Activities

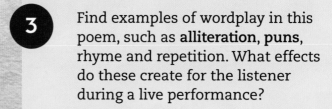

1 Think of a time when someone made you feel positive and valued. Describe what happened and how it felt.

The poem opposite is by a slam performance poet, which means it is delivered live to an audience. The text is a transcript (a written version of what was said). Read it aloud, thinking about where it takes place and how the poet 'plays' with words to entertain the reader.

2 In the poem the poet experiences a range of feelings in school.

Identify at least three of these feelings. How far can you empathize (share an understanding) with any of them?

3 Find examples of wordplay in this poem, such as **alliteration**, **puns**, rhyme and repetition. What effects do these create for the listener during a live performance?

4 What is noticeably different about a slam poem? Support your ideas with reference to particular words or phrases that Dreadlock Alien uses.

Think about layout, **slang** and informal words or phrases.

5 In pairs or small groups read the poem again. This time make it your own by performing it with expression and gestures. You could change some of the words or add in sound effects.

🕐 Extra Time

Summarize the main message of this poem in a **tweet**, using no more than 140 characters.

'Well Done'
by Dreadlock Alien

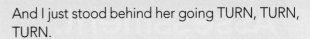

Six years old.

And no one had ever told me I was good at something,

but one time, let me tell you about, that got my heart jumping.

Let me take you right back to the start.

I loved Mrs Evans because she taught me for art.

Most lessons I sat around because I thought they were boring.

Me and my mate did an impression of someone snoring,

I got sent outside the class, paper and pencil we did some withdrawing.

Not well looked after, but I was full of laughter, I was always trying to be dafter than Darren on the next table.

Sometimes life was like my desk... a little bit unstable.

So there I am sat outside the classroom again.

Only got one pencil because I'm not allowed a pen but I can...

doodle a poodle, I can draw more than a score.

I can sketch someone sketchy, I can paint the front door.

I can scribble in dribble, I can create a cartoon.

I can even draw the curtains bruv, to rub out the moon.

The paper, the pencil and me.

Sometimes my efforts were blunt, up front, sharply spoken but I kept a clear mind.

See I used up ten pencils in one day!

Not because I wrote a lot but because I sharpened them all away.

Mrs Evans was at the front telling everybody learn, learn, learn.

And I just stood behind her going TURN, TURN, TURN.

See I loved art lessons, 'cause learning was fun,

especially when I got my work back and it said... Well Done!

Oh no, jelly belly, had this weird feeling inside.

Teacher said you better watch out boy before you burst with pride.

I said 'Oh no, Mrs Evans I don't like this feeling.'

And I wet myself and cried.

So when people say well done I tend to shy away.

But you can always rest assured I'll remember what you say.

So whether you're a teacher, a social worker or a mum.

Just remember the importance of telling the young ones...

Well done!

And in the future when it may seem that they're swimming against the tide.

They'll look back to those few seconds and how it made them feel so good inside.

📖 Glossary

alliteration repetition of the same letter or sound at the beginning of words, e.g sitting silently

pun a type of joke that plays on the two meanings of a word

slang informal words typically used by specific groups but not in a specific geographical area

tweet a short message with a maximum of 140 characters used in the social networking site Twitter

10 Assessment: Reading, Analysing and Recommending Poems for Public Display

📖 Glossary

Standard English the variety of English that is regarded as 'correct' and is used in more formal situations. It is not specific to any geographical area and can be spoken or written.

Your local community is planning to run a poetry project called 'Who We Are'. The project will display (and play) poems in public places, such as school foyers, bus stops, cafés, shopping malls and sports centres. All the poems should reflect the theme of identity, saying something meaningful to ordinary people, but in an interesting way. They could be about friends, relationships, choices, family, appearance or anything else that is linked to 'who we are'.

Your task is to read a selection of poems and choose one for display. You will need to write a letter or email to the leader of the project to explain your choice.

Before you choose…

Read the three poems on page 59 and consider the questions below.

- What is this poem about?

- How are its theme and message relevant?

- Why might people like the structure or form of the poem?

- What poetic devices does it use and what impact do these have on the reader/listener?

- How might people feel after reading or hearing this poem?

When you have chosen…

Write an email or letter to the leader of the project, analysing the poem and explaining why you think it should be displayed.

Your letter/email should be written in **Standard English**, starting '*Dear Mr Bolton*' and ending '*Yours sincerely*'.

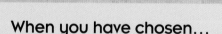

Note that, for the purposes of this assessment, you will be marked on your reading and analysis skills, not on your writing skills.

'Scaffolding'
by Seamus Heaney

Masons, when they start upon a building,
Are careful to test out the scaffolding;

Make sure that planks won't slip at busy points,
Secure all ladders, tighten bolted joints.

And yet all this comes down when the job's done
Showing off walls of sure and solid stone.

So if, my dear, there sometimes seems to be
Old bridges breaking between you and me

Never fear. We may let the scaffolds fall
Confident that we have built our wall.

Extract from 'Cannibal Kids'
by Kate Tempest

Round here,
These cannibal kids want to be kings
They don't know that kindness is courage
Or that sympathy sings
Much louder than violence
They are bitter and drained
Eyes of ice stare from figures of flames
Puff-chested, restless, nameless,
They carry their pain
To the point of being painless.

'The Road Not Taken'
by Robert Frost

Two roads diverged in a yellow wood,
And sorry I could not travel both
And be one traveler, long I stood
And looked down one as far as I could
To where it bent in the undergrowth;

Then took the other, as just as fair,
And having perhaps the better claim
Because it was grassy and wanted wear,
Though as for that the passing there
Had worn them really about the same,

And both that morning equally lay
In leaves no step had trodden black.
Oh, I marked the first for another day!
Yet knowing how way leads on to way
I doubted if I should ever come back.

I shall be telling this with a sigh
Somewhere ages and ages hence:
Two roads diverged in a wood, and I,
I took the one less traveled by,
And that has made all the difference.

3

OUT OF THIS WORLD

WHAT WILL THE FUTURE LOOK LIKE?

Introduction

All good science fiction asks questions: What will the future look like? Will our lives be better or worse in the future? How will we cope with change?

Science-fiction stories have already predicted many things that have become a reality, such as mobile phones, robots and the Internet. What they couldn't always predict accurately were the consequences of these inventions and the effects on people's lives and on our planet.

Science-fiction writers explore the question 'What if…?', looking beyond the new inventions and new events, and show how we might cope with them.

ignite INTERVIEW
Jaine Fenn, Science-fiction writer

Science fiction is the fiction of the possible. You can do anything. You can tell a story that can happen anywhere in the universe and you can change any of the rules. You can throw in aliens. You can throw in inventions. We are always going to want to know what is happening in the future and science fiction is the best way to explore what might or might not happen in the future. Imagination is the main ingredient of science fiction, taking a step out of the ordinary world. However, you have to remember the person's story, the character, all the way through.

Activities

1 List science-fiction films, TV programmes and books that you already know, e.g. *Avatar*, *Doctor Who* and *The Invisible Man*.

2 Using one example from your list, pick out something that is different in the future and explain it to your partner.

3 Discuss what you think the future will look like.

1 What is Science Fiction?

↻ Objective

Recognize the typical features of science fiction.

ignite INTERVIEW

'With a science-fiction story, the first thing that comes along is nearly always the idea, the "what if…".'

Jaine Fenn

People have always wondered about the future. It's human nature to be adventurous, to invent new things and to explore new places and ideas, but also to be afraid of change and the unknown. Science-fiction writers combine these human instincts to create gripping and thought-provoking stories.

Science fiction tends to fall into one or more of these categories:

- a global disaster: either man-made or natural
- travel: beyond our planet or in time
- the arrival of aliens on our planet
- a scientific discovery or technological advance that changes lives
- characters with superpowers.

✎ Activities

1. Decide which of the science-fiction films, television programmes and stories you know would fit into the categories above. Note that some may fit into more than one category.

A blurb is the short description that appears on the back of a book. It tells you what the story is about and also tries to persuade you to buy the book. Read the blurbs on the right, all of which are from science-fiction stories.

2 Which category of science fiction do you think each blurb describes?

3 Publishers can make blurbs exciting through vocabulary choices, verb tenses (such as the **present tense**) and punctuation. Pick out some examples of these from each of the blurbs on the right and explain their effect.

SPAG

4 Based on these three blurbs, which of these books would you most like to read and why? Give examples of specific words or phrases that hooked you in.

📖 Glossary

present tense   a verb that describes something that is happening now, e.g. *I run, you wake, he walks, they talk*

past tense   a verb that describes something that happened earlier, e.g. *he arrived, I lost, you called, they helped*

🕐 Extra Time

Read some blurbs from other books (including this book!). To what extent do they work in the same way as the science-fiction blurbs on this page?

A: Blurb from *Contact* by Carl Sagan

At first it seemed impossible – a radio signal that came not from Earth but from far beyond the nearest stars. But then the signal was translated, and what had been impossible became terrifying…

For the signal contains the information to build a Machine that can travel to the stars. A Machine that can take a human to meet those that sent the message.

They are eager to meet us: they have been watching and waiting for a long time.

And now they will judge.

B: Blurb from a play adaptation of *The Invisible Man* by H. G. Wells

Through the biting cold of the year's last snowfall, a strange man arrives at a village inn, his eyes concealed by dark glasses and his face and hands covered in bandages. Griffin, the new guest at the Coach and Horses, hides a chilling secret – he has developed a formula that has made him invisible, and will stop at nothing in his desperate struggle to find the antidote and keep his discovery safe.

C: Blurb from *The Day of the Triffids* by John Wyndham

When Bill Masen wakes up blindfolded in hospital, there is bitter irony in his situation. Carefully removing his bandages, he realizes that he is the only person who can see: everyone else, doctors and patients alike, have been blinded by a meteor shower. Now, with civilization in chaos, the triffids – huge, venomous, large-rooted plants able to 'walk', feeding on human flesh – can have their day.

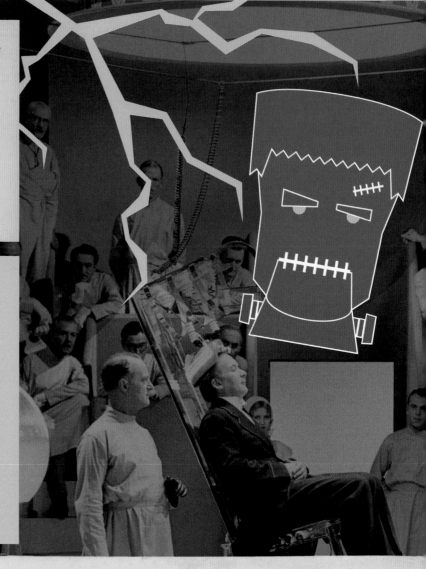

② Frankenstein's Monster

↻ Objective

Explore the build-up of atmosphere and tension.

Many science-fiction stories focus on the theme of people creating something, or some being, that they cannot control. In the 19th century, Mary Shelley wrote the story about Dr Frankenstein creating a monster without foreseeing the terrible consequences of his creation, both for people and the monster itself.

Read this extract, which describes the moment when Frankenstein's monster comes to life. Think about the techniques the writer uses to create atmosphere and tension.

Extract from *Frankenstein*

by Mary Shelley

It was on a dreary night of November, that I beheld the accomplishment of my **toils**. With an anxiety that almost amounted to agony, I collected the instruments of life around me, that I might **infuse** a spark of being into the lifeless thing that lay at my feet. It was already one in the morning; the rain pattered dismally against the panes, and my candle was nearly burnt out, when, by the glimmer of the half-extinguished light, I saw the dull yellow eye of the creature open; it breathed hard, and a **convulsive** motion agitated its limbs.

How can I describe my emotions at this **catastrophe**, or **delineate** the wretch whom with such **infinite** pains and care I had **endeavoured** to form? His limbs were in proportion, and I had selected his features as beautiful. Beautiful! – Great God! His yellow skin scarcely covered the work of muscles and arteries beneath; his hair was of a **lustrous** black, and flowing; his teeth of pearly whiteness; but these luxuriances only formed a more horrid contrast with his watery eyes, that seemed almost of the same colour as the **dun**-white sockets in which they were set, his shrivelled complexion and straight black lips.

✎ Activities

1a In the first paragraph, the writer draws the reader into the scene by describing the time, the season, the light and the sounds in the room. Think of three **adjectives** to sum up the scene and explain why you chose them. **SPAG**

1b What do we learn about Dr Frankenstein's state of mind in this first paragraph? How does it add to the tension and suspense for the reader?

2 What does Dr Frankenstein think of his creation? Select at least three words or phrases, for example 'the lifeless thing', and explain what they tell us about Dr Frankenstein's attitude to his creation.

3 How does the writer use punctuation to show the narrator's emotions? **SPAG**

4 Dr Frankenstein explains that he tried to make the creature beautiful.

a List four features he describes in a positive way.

b List four features he describes in a negative way.

c What type of body is hinted at by the negative descriptions?

5 Now write the opening to your own science-fiction story about a creation. Using what you have learnt in this lesson, concentrate on:

- how to draw the reader in
- creating tension
- using punctuation for effect.

⬧ Support

Think carefully about the effect of question marks, exclamation marks and dashes.

↔ Stretch

The writer uses semi-colons in two different ways in this extract. Explain both uses. How do the semi-colons contribute to the effect of the description on the reader?

📖 Glossary

toils work

infuse force in, mix

convulsive jerky

catastrophe disaster

delineate explain

infinite vast, never-ending

endeavoured tried

lustrous glossy

dun dull grey brown

adjective a word that describes a noun, e.g. *happy, blue, furious*

🕒 Extra Time

Frankenstein caused a lot of argument because it challenged the idea that only God creates life. Mary Shelley was an unusual woman for her time. Find out more about her life and work.

③ Science and Humour in Science Fiction

↻ Objective

Understand how vocabulary and language are used in science fiction.

Science-fiction stories can ask some serious questions: about us, about our planet, about the choices we make and the way we behave, particularly in times of crisis. But science fiction can also be great fun, often created through the use of scientific inventions and humour.

✎ Activities

1 Read the extracts opposite. They are from the script of a TV episode of *Doctor Who*.

Doctor Who stories are always packed full of classic science-fiction themes, such as aliens and amazing scientific inventions. Where do these themes appear in these extracts? Can you identify any other themes?

Margaret is an alien, a Slitheen, who is in disguise as Lord Mayor. She is behaving suspiciously so the Doctor pays her a visit. Margaret flees, but the Doctor and his companions give chase.

Extract 1

Extract from a *Doctor Who* script

*CUT TO Margaret, still running, but as she does so, she's clipping her brooch and the two earrings together, so they become a gizmo. And grinning, she presses them, ka-chick – Margaret vanishes. No **FX**, just an instant blink, gone.*

CUT TO Captain Jack, outraged, the Doctor and Rose calm.

CAPTAIN JACK
  Teleport! She's got a teleport! That's cheating, now we're never gonna get her –

ROSE
  Ohh, the Doctor's very good with teleports.

The Doctor smiles, holds up the sonic screwdriver, whirrs. Margaret blinks into existence, much closer to the Doctor and the others, now – but in the blink, she's been switched round, so that she's now running towards them!

She stops, realises this, horrified – about turns, runs away – on the hoof, she presses her device, ka-chick – Margaret vanishes.

The Doctor whirrs. Margaret reappears, running towards them. And now she's knackered, gasping for breath, stops. (As Mickey, running, finally reaches them.)

THE DOCTOR
  I could do this all day.

MARGARET
  I couldn't.
(puts hands up)
  This is persecution, why can't you leave me alone? What did I ever do to you?

THE DOCTOR
  You tried to kill me and destroy this entire planet.

MARGARET
  Apart from that?

In the next scene, the Doctor, Rose, Captain Jack, Mickey and Margaret are all in the Town Hall, looking at a model city. The Doctor is trying to work out what Margaret (the Slitheen) is up to.

Extract 2

Extract from a *Doctor Who* script

THE DOCTOR
(studying the model)
> This station is designed to explode, the moment it reaches capacity.
> [...]

The Doctor has prised his fingers under the model, hauls up a panel – the model buildings go flying, as the panel lifts up in a neat, solid, flat 2ft x 4ft. Underneath, it's a giant circuit board – intricate metal patterns, a **motherboard**.

THE DOCTOR
> Fantastic!

CAPTAIN JACK
(awestruck)
> ... Is that a tribophysical waveform macro-kinetic extrapolator?

THE DOCTOR
> Couldn't put it better myself. Look at it! The workmanship!

He rips it free, hands it to Jack. (Then lose the Doctor b/g; he wanders off, seeing something more interesting...)

CAPTAIN JACK
> Genius! You didn't build that?

MARGARET
> I have my hobbies. A little tinkering.

CAPTAIN JACK
> No, I mean you *really* didn't build that. Way beyond you.

MICKEY
> I bet she stole it.

MARGARET
> It fell into my hands.

ROSE
> Is it a weapon?

CAPTAIN JACK
> It's transport! Y'see, the reactor blows up, the rift opens, phenomenal cosmic disaster, but this thing shrouds you in a forcefield, you've got this energy bubble, zzhum, all around you, so you're safe – then you just feed it coordinates, stand on top, and ride the concussion, way out of the solar system –

MICKEY
> It's a surfboard!

CAPTAIN JACK
> A pan-dimensional surfboard, yup.

MARGARET
> And it would've worked. I'd have surfed away from this dead-end dump and back to civilisation.

MICKEY
> You'd blow up a planet? Just to get a lift?

MARGARET
> Like stepping on an anthill.

📖 Glossary

FX special effects

teleport technology enabling a person to disappear from one place and appear in another

motherboard the place that holds a computer's microprocessor chip and everything that connects to it

b/g background

More to explore

In science fiction, writers can let their imaginations create all sorts of amazing gadgets that enable characters to do surprising and amazing things. This can be very entertaining for the reader.

✎ Activities continued

2a Pick out an item in the extracts on pages 66–67 that uses advanced science or technology. Explain what you think it might look like and what it does.

2b The description 'sonic screwdriver' uses two words that are familiar to us, but their combination is surprising. Look at the description 'tribophysical waveform macro-kinetic extrapolator'. What parts of this description do you recognize? Use a dictionary to explore any words that are unfamiliar. Does it make any sense or is the writer just having fun?

3 Make up another gadget or gizmo that could be used in a science-fiction story. Decide what it can do and give it a name that includes some scientific-sounding words.

▧ Support

Use words such as thermal, dynamic, magnetic, micro, atomic, nuclear and combine them with some ordinary-sounding words to describe your gadget.

↔ Stretch

Look up the meaning of acoustic, biometric, polymorphic and cryogenic. Think of a gadget that could be described using some of these words.

One of the reasons *Doctor Who* is so popular is that it is very funny. Science fiction gives writers the freedom to imagine strange and bizarre characters, who say things that are totally unexpected and act in surprising ways.

4 In pairs, make up a short comedy scene involving the Doctor and an alien. You will need to include a scientific invention and some humour. Follow the steps below.

1
Think carefully about each character. The Doctor is clever, brave, truthful and agile, for example. Is your alien evil, shy or clumsy?

2
Imagine the Doctor has a new gadget that he is showing to the alien. What might this gadget do?

3
How might the alien respond? Would it be afraid, angry or confused? What might happen next?

4
Write a short script. Stage directions (which tell the actor what to do or state when something else happens on stage) can be included in brackets. For example:

GRANT

How much time do we have?
(Looks at his watch)

5
If there is time, act out your comedy scene. Think carefully about your expressions, gestures and how you will say your lines. If you are including slapstick comedy, you will have to work out your moves carefully.

☑ Progress Check

Give your script to another pair or perform your scene in front of another pair. Ask them to give you two ratings, on a scale of 1 to 5, with 5 being the highest, on:

- your idea for a scientific gadget
- the humour in your writing/performance.

4 Robot: Friend or Foe?

↺ Objective

Investigate different ideas and points of view.

Science-fiction writers have always been fascinated by the role that robots might play in our lives in the future. But will robots be helpful companions or could they become our arch-enemies? If we make them clever, will they become too clever and end up controlling us? And do robots have rights and feelings?

The following headline and summary appeared in the *MailOnline* news website in November 2012.

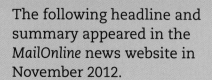

Rise of the Machines: Autonomous killer robots 'could be developed in 20 years'

- Militaries around the world 'very excited' about replacing soldiers with robots that can act independently.
- U.S. leads the way with automated weapons systems, but **drones** still need remote control operator authorisation to open fire.
- Human Rights Watch calls for worldwide ban on autonomous killing machines before governments start using them.

✎ Activities

1 List as many robots as you can from stories, films, TV shows or games. Explain whether these robots are friends and helpers for humans, or are evil beings that are enemies of humans.

2 Choose one of these robots and write a short paragraph explaining the role it plays in the science-fiction story. For example, 'In the film *Forbidden Planet*, *Robby the Robot helps the spaceship crew to...*'.

3 With a partner, talk about the pros and cons of using drones instead of soldiers. Consider the following questions:

- According to the extract, what can the robots do? What can't they do?
- Why do you think military organizations might want to replace soldiers with robots?
- Why do you think Human Rights Watch has called for a ban on autonomous killing machines?

Isaac Asimov wrote many stories about robots. He imagined a time when robots were programmed to obey these three strict laws:

The Three Laws

1. A robot may not injure a human being or, through inaction, allow a human being to come to harm.

2. A robot must obey the orders given to it by human beings, except where such orders would conflict with the First Law.

3. A robot must protect its own existence as long as such protection does not conflict with the First or Second Laws.

Asimov's stories explored how clever robots might become and how they might become more like humans. The ideas in some of his robot stories were developed later in a film called *I, Robot*.

4 The three laws were supposed to keep humans safe, but what could happen if a robot was incorrectly programmed?

📖 Glossary

drone   a robotic device that is remotely controlled by humans

pronoun   a word used instead of a noun

first-person narrative   story told by a character, using the words 'I' and 'we'

colleague   person you work with

programmer   computer scientist who makes computer systems work

experimental model   trial or practice computer program

5 Read the extract below. Most science-fiction stories are told from the point of view of humans, but in this one, it is the computer that is the narrator. Identify the **pronouns** that show this is a **first-person narrative**.

SPAG

Extract from 'True Love' by Isaac Asimov

My name is Joe. That is what my **colleague**, Milton Davidson, calls me. He is a **programmer** and I am a computer program. I am part of the Multivac-complex and am connected with other parts all over the world. I know everything. Almost everything.

I am Milton's private program. His Joe. He understands more about programming than anyone in the world, and I am his **experimental model**. He has made me speak better than any other computer can.

6 Imagine you are a robot that does not obey Asimov's three laws. Perhaps you have a design flaw or your circuits have been damaged. Write an email to a fellow robot describing an incident where you have broken one or more of Asimov's laws.

5 Cloning: Cool or Cruel?

↻ Objective

Prepare and present a viewpoint for a debate.

Science-fiction stories sometimes explore difficult decisions that people have to make about new scientific advances. These advances can improve the quality of many lives (e.g. medication and energy resources), but they can also have negative effects or be used for the wrong purposes.

1996 → DOLLY

In 1996, Dolly the sheep was born. She was the first cloned mammal: an exact **genetic** copy of another sheep. Since then, cloning has caused a lot of debate. Many people worry about the possibility of cloning a human being. Would a human clone be an individual, even though they were the exact copy of someone else?

who are ewe?

who are we?!

✎ Activities

1a The extract below comes from the science-fiction novel *Unique*, which tells the traumatic story of Dominic, who discovers he is a clone, created from the cells of his dead brother. The extract explains how the media revealed the illegal genetic work done by Dr Wishart. As you read the extract, decide whether the writer seems sympathetic to cloning or not.

Extract from *Unique* by Alison Allen-Gray

All sorts of things had come out about what Wishart had promised his customers, how he could guarantee that their baby would be just as they wanted it. He'd started with the gene-screens, selecting the right eye colour, the right IQ, or saying he could guarantee that the 'outcome' would be a fast runner or good at music. And then he'd gone for the big one – an 'entire' cloned baby. You can have yourself copied, he'd boasted in one recorded phone conversation. No one would ever know – after all, how many kids bear an uncanny resemblance to one or other of their parents?

1b What does the use of the word 'boasted' tell us about Dr Wishart? What does the phrase 'gone for the big one' imply about cloning?

2 Imagine you are a clone. How might it make you feel? List the possible advantages and disadvantages of being a clone.

Read the following two extracts, which both focus on the cloning of animals. The first, below, is from a news website. The second, page 74, is from the organization Compassion, a charity that campaigns against cloning.

Scientists in Brasília have come up with a groundbreaking way to ensure the survival of endangered **species**: cloning them. Scientists working on the project, which is a partnership between government agricultural research agency EMBRAPA and Brasília Zoological Garden, have already successfully cloned cows and horses.

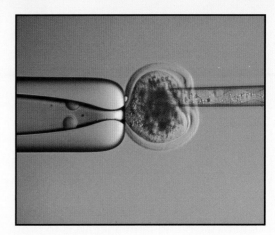

Now they are turning their attention to eight at-risk species: jaguar, collared anteaters, maned wolves, bush dogs, black lion tamarin monkeys, gray brocket deer, Brazilian aardvarks (known as coatis) and bisons.

For the past two years, scientists have been collecting genetic samples from animals native to the Cerrado, the vast savannah surrounding Brasília, and storing them in a **DNA** bank.

Once the zoo has received the go ahead from government agencies, researchers will be trained in adapting the technique of cloning to wild animals. Researchers predict that the first successful clone will be a maned wolf, the species for which they have the most DNA samples.

The animals will supply zoos. There are no plans to release the clones into the wild, as interbreeding with clones would decrease the species' overall genetic variation. A healthy wild population needs to have a diverse gene pool to resist disease.

📖 Glossary

genetic to do with characteristics inherited from parents

species a type or particular group of animals

DNA deoxyribonucleic acid, a substance found in living cells that stores genetic information

More to explore

CLONING = CRUELTY

Compassion is against the cloning of animals for food. Compassion has been campaigning in the EU and in the UK against cloning for a number of years.

The aim of cloning farm animals is to produce replicas of the animals with the highest economic value, for example the fastest-growing pigs or the **highest-yielding** dairy cows; however, the process of cloning itself causes animal suffering and the animals with the highest economic value are prone to developing severe health problems. Pushed to their physical limits, they are condemned to a lifetime of suffering.

The case against cloning

The Cloning = Cruelty campaign highlights the **intrinsic** animal welfare issues of selective breeding in animals for food, i.e. meat and dairy. Research also shows that many cloned farm animals are born with deformed organs, and live short and miserable lives.

Animals involved in the cloning process suffer

The cloning of farm animals can involve great suffering. A cloned **embryo** has to be implanted into a surrogate mother who carries it to birth. Cloned embryos tend to be large and can result in painful births that are often carried out by Caesarean section. Many clones die during pregnancy or birth. Of those that survive, a significant proportion die in the early days and weeks of life from problems such as heart, liver and kidney failure.

📖 Glossary

highest-yielding most productive

intrinsic essential

embryo a baby or young animal starting to grow in the womb

tone the way words are spoken, e.g. in a serious tone, a light-hearted tone, etc.

✎ Activities continued

3 Prepare to debate the following question:

Should scientists be allowed to experiment with cloning for the benefit of animals, humans and a better future?

Follow the steps below to prepare your viewpoint.

1 **With a partner, talk about the following questions, using points and examples from the two extracts about cloning.**

- Why are scientists looking into the possibility of cloning wild animals?

- How will that help the animal population in the wild?

- How will that help zoos?

- Why is Compassion against cloning?

2 **Decide if you will argue for or against cloning, then list your arguments.**

If possible, do some research on the Internet or in the library. Think about the possible uses of cloned body parts and why some religions may be against cloning.

3 **Write a presentation.**

Using the arguments you have listed, write a presentation that you will give in the debate, outlining your views and giving reasons for them.

Back up your arguments with examples and references from what you have learned in this unit or from your own research.

4 **Rehearse your presentation, speaking clearly and slowly.**

Stand still, but make sure you look up from your notes, so that you make eye contact with your audience. Use pauses and variations in your **tone** and volume to give emphasis to what you say.

5 **Present your viewpoint (either in a full class debate or to your partner).**

⬙ Support

Remember to use the ideas from the articles and your answers to the questions. Begin: *I am against (or for) cloning because…*

↔ Stretch

Try to anticipate the arguments used on the other side and think of ways to argue back, using words and phrases such as 'Even though', 'However', 'More importantly', 'On the other hand'.

6 Aliens!

↻ Objective

Recognize the techniques used to create effective description.

The idea of aliens has always fascinated science-fiction writers and film-makers. Whether they are hostile, friendly, funny or cute, alien characters often prompt us to ask questions about our own humanity.

✎ Activities

1 What do you imagine when you think of an alien? Describe it, and discuss whether you think an alien coming to our planet is likely to be friendly or hostile. Would we be friendly or hostile towards aliens if we encountered them?

The science-fiction novel *The War of the Worlds* explored what might happen if aliens invaded our planet. H. G. Wells wrote the novel in 1898, a time when Britain had invaded and colonized many countries.

Read the extract on page 77.

2a Notice how the writer makes us wait to see the alien and, when it does emerge, it is bit by bit. What is the effect of this delay on the reader?

2b Why do you think the writer compares part of the alien to a snake? The tentacles are also described as 'Gorgon' (a monster in Greek mythology with snakes for hair). Why does the writer do this?

2c Look at how the writer describes the alien's movements. Look closely at the **verbs** (e.g. 'writhing') and **adverbs** (e.g. 'painfully') the writer has chosen. What do they suggest about the alien? How does this influence our (and the narrator's) reaction to it?

SPAG

3 Imagine an alien spaceship has arrived in your school grounds over the weekend. Describe what might emerge on Monday morning. Use some of the descriptive techniques explored in Activities 2a–c.

- Describe the alien, in detail, as it emerges.
- Describe how the alien looks, moves, sounds and smells.
- Use comparisons and images to suggest aspects of your alien's character.
- Show the reactions of the people watching.

In this extract, the narrator describes the opening of one of many cylinders that have dropped from the sky into London. The cylinders are from Mars, which is a dying planet in the story.

Extract from *The War of the Worlds* by H. G. Wells

I think everyone expected to see a man emerge – possibly something a little unlike us **terrestrial** men, but in all essentials a man. I know I did. But, looking, I presently saw something stirring within the shadow: greyish billowy movements, one above another, and then two luminous discs – like eyes. Then something resembling a little grey snake, about the thickness of a walking-stick, coiled up out of the writhing middle, and wriggled in the air towards me – and then another.

A sudden chill came over me. There was a loud shriek from a woman behind. I half turned, keeping my eyes fixed on the cylinder still, from which other tentacles were now projecting, and began pushing my way back from the edge of the pit. I saw astonishment giving place to horror on the faces of the people around me. I heard inarticulate explanations on all sides. There was a general movement backwards. I saw the shopman struggling on the edge of the pit. I found myself alone, and saw the people on the other side of the pit running off, Stent among them. I looked again at the cylinder, and ungovernable terror gripped me. I stood petrified and staring.

A big greyish rounded bulk, the size, perhaps of a bear, was rising slowly and painfully out of the cylinder. As it bulged up and caught the light, it glistened like wet leather.

Two large dark-coloured eyes were regarding me steadfastly. The mass that framed them, the head of the thing, was rounded, and had, one might say, a face.

There was a mouth under the eyes, the lipless brim of which quivered and panted, and dropped saliva. The whole creature heaved and pulsated convulsively. A **lank** tentacular **appendage** gripped the edge of the cylinder, another swayed in the air.

Those who have never seen a living Martian can scarcely imagine the horror of its appearance. The peculiar V-shaped mouth with its pointed upper lip, the absence of brow ridges, the absence of a chin beneath the wedge-like lower lip, the incessant quivering of this mouth, the Gorgon groups of tentacles, the **tumultuous** breathing of the lungs in a strange atmosphere, the evident painfulness of movement due to the greater gravitational energy of the earth – above all the extraordinary intensity of the eyes – were at once vital, intense, inhuman, crippled and monstrous. There was something **fungoid** in the oily brown skin, something in the clumsy deliberation of the tedious movements unspeakably nasty. Even at this first encounter, this first glimpse, I was overcome with disgust and dread.

📖 Glossary

verbs 'doing' or action words, e.g. *ran, laughed, screamed*

adverbs words which describe how an action is carried out, e.g. *happily, angrily*

terrestrial from Earth

lank limp

appendage a thing that forms part of something larger

tumultuous noisy and excited

fungoid like a fungus

7 The End of the World?

↻ Objective

Explore the features of a good story opening and use them effectively.

Many science-fiction stories explore how our world might change in a drastic way, for example because of environmental changes or destruction by powerful weapons. These stories focus on how people might cope with such devastating changes. Read the extract below and then complete Activities 1a–1c.

Extract from the opening of *Exodus* by Julie Bertagna

WING

Midwinter 2099

Earth spins. And Wing, the high island, is hurled into the sunless shadow of night.

It's just a minute past three.

The people of Wing are gathering in what's left of their village. Downhill, the salty, sea-lashed streets run straight into churning, cold-boiled ocean. The oldest islanders can remember a time when Wing's folding hills sheered away to sandstone cliffs that plunged on to a wide and rocky shore. The clifftops were still visible at ebb tide last summer, haunting the waves with their dark shadows.

Now it's all ocean.

✎ Activities

1a Which words suggest that something negative has happened?

1b Identify three short sentences, for example 'Now it's all ocean', and explain how they are used and the effect the sentences have. **SPAG**

1c What dangers and problems do the people have to face?

ignite INTERVIEW

'Think about what you can do dramatically, at the beginning, to make sure that the person that is reading this thinks "Wow, this is interesting".'

Jaine Fenn

Read this opening of Philip Reeve's science-fiction novel *Mortal Engines*, which is set after a devastating nuclear war and geological changes on Earth.

Extract from *Mortal Engines* by Philip Reeve

It was a dark, blustery afternoon in spring, and the city of London was chasing a small mining town across the dried-out bed of the old North Sea.

In happier times, London would never have bothered with such feeble prey. The great Traction City had once spent its days hunting far bigger towns than this, ranging north as far as the edges of the Ice Waste and south to the shores of the Mediterranean. But lately prey of any kind had started to grow scarce, and some of the larger cities had begun to look hungrily at London.

2a What surprises you about the description of London in the first line?

2b How do you think London is able to run across the dry sea bed? What would need to be different about London?

2c What images and animals do you think of when you read the word 'prey'? How can a city be like a predator or prey?

3 Write the opening paragraphs of a new science-fiction story. Imagine there has just been (or there is about to be) a disaster. Include:

- a description of a place and/or group of people

- surprising images and comparisons

- hints and clues that something is about to happen or has just happened

- ideas that will make the reader ask questions about what is happening

- an ordinary place described as if it is extraordinary.

Imagine the place where you live. What would be different after a disaster? Describe how the streets, houses and people are different.

↔ Stretch   SPAG

Have you used different types of sentences and punctuation for effect? How can you make the place you have described seem even more extraordinary? Rewrite your opening sentences to include different types of sentences and an even more extraordinary image.

☑ Progress Check

How confident do you now feel that you can use these features effectively when writing the opening to another science-fiction story?

8 Superheroes

↻ Objectives

Use inference and deduction.

Superheroes often play a key role in science-fiction stories. Some of the first, such as Superman, Batman and Green Lantern, were created for comics, although they are now also in films, books and games. But how do we know the real meaning behind the images and what the characters are saying?

Inference involves working out, or deducing, the real meaning behind the words and images by using clues from the text, speech or pictures. You need to be a detective when reading, watching and listening. You are looking for subtle or hidden meaning and clues.

When you listen to someone speak, you should look out for what they really mean, for example:

'What time will you be back?' Mum shouted just before I left.

'I don't know!' I called, while hurriedly stuffing the time-extrapolator into my already bulging rucksack.

I don't want to come back early or end up arguing about what time I'm going to be back. Also, I REALLY don't want to tell you what I'm up to.

I want to know you are safe and that you are not out late at night.

This extract comes from a Superman comic.

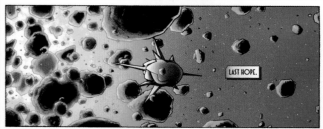

✎ Activities

1 Taking any superhero that you're familiar with, explain how what they appear like on the surface might differ from who they really are.

2 In your own words, explain where Superman came from, making inferences from the comic extract.

This very short comic strip comes from *The Phoenix* comic.

3 Using your skills of inference and deduction, talk about the events in this short comic strip. Consider the questions below.

- What can you work out about the main character?

- What can you assume about the Crystal Gibbon of Cathay?

- What you can deduce about the volcano?

- What do you think is likely to happen next?

📖 Glossary

dialogue   conversation between two or more characters

4 Write a short piece of **dialogue** that could be used in a science-fiction story.

- Make sure the reader has to use inference and deduction to work out what is really being said.

- Use thought bubbles to show what the characters are really thinking and saying.

- Write at least five lines and include two characters.

📑 Support

Using the example on page 80, imagine that Mum has just walked into the room while you are hiding something behind your back. Continue the conversation.

9 New Worlds

↺ Objectives

Recognize the impact of settings.

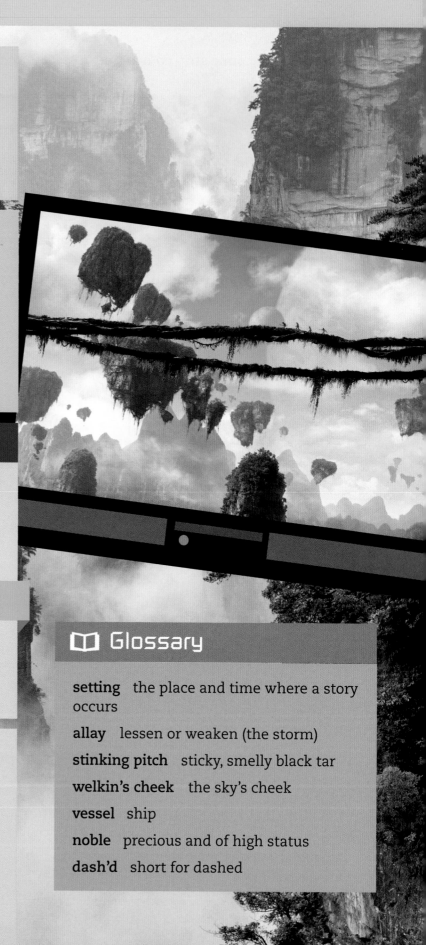

Travel is a theme in many science-fiction stories. It can be time travel, space travel or even virtual travel. The film *Avatar* follows the story of human invasion of another planet to exploit its resources. Most of the action takes place on the beautiful lush planet of Pandora, which is rich in resources and whose inhabitants live in harmony with their environment.

✎ Activities

1a The **setting** of Pandora at the beginning of *Avatar* is very different to our own world. What words come to mind when you look at the picture on the right?

↔ Stretch

Consider how events in the film, such as taking over someone else's land, reflect real historical events or social issues.

1b The setting can often help create the atmosphere of a science-fiction story. Suggest a suitable setting for each of the following possible atmospheres:

- dark and menacing
- peaceful
- uneasy
- friendly.

📖 Glossary

setting   the place and time where a story occurs

allay   lessen or weaken (the storm)

stinking pitch   sticky, smelly black tar

welkin's cheek   the sky's cheek

vessel   ship

noble   precious and of high status

dash'd   short for dashed

Shakespeare's play *The Tempest* is sometimes described as science fiction and has inspired other science-fiction stories and films. Although it was written around 400 years ago, it includes characters with superhuman powers and people travelling to unknown, isolated places and taking command over native inhabitants.

The Tempest opens dramatically in the middle of a raging storm. Miranda, daughter of the magician Prospero, pleads with her father to quell the terrible storm.

Extract from *The Tempest* by William Shakespeare

Miranda   If by your art, my dearest father, you have

Put the wild waters in this roar, **allay** them.

The sky, it seems, would pour down **stinking pitch**,

But that the sea, mounting to th'**welkin's cheek**,

Dashes the fire out. O, I have suffered

With those that I saw suffer! A brave **vessel**,

Who had no doubt some **noble** creature in her,

Dash'd all to pieces!

2a Write down the clues that show there is a storm.

2b What is Shakespeare comparing the sea to in 'Wild waters in this roar'? What does it make you think about the storm?

2c Why do you think Shakespeare chose a storm for the opening of *The Tempest*? What is the effect of this setting?

2d This is a very visual piece of writing. If Miranda's words were turned into a film version, what would you see?

3 In your assessment task (on pages 84–85), you will be writing the opening of a science-fiction story. To help prepare for that, start to think about the possible setting for your story.

Use the questions below to plan your ideas.

What is different in this place and time?

What hints are there that things could get better or worse?

Are there any signs of other life?

What dangers are in this place?

What is the weather like?

How is your setting important to your story?

Who or what is in control?

What will make your setting seem important and dramatic?

⏱ Extra Time

List other science-fiction settings that you know from films, television programmes or books. What do the settings tell you?

10 Assessment: Writing the Opening of a Science-Fiction Story

Plan, draft, edit and proofread.

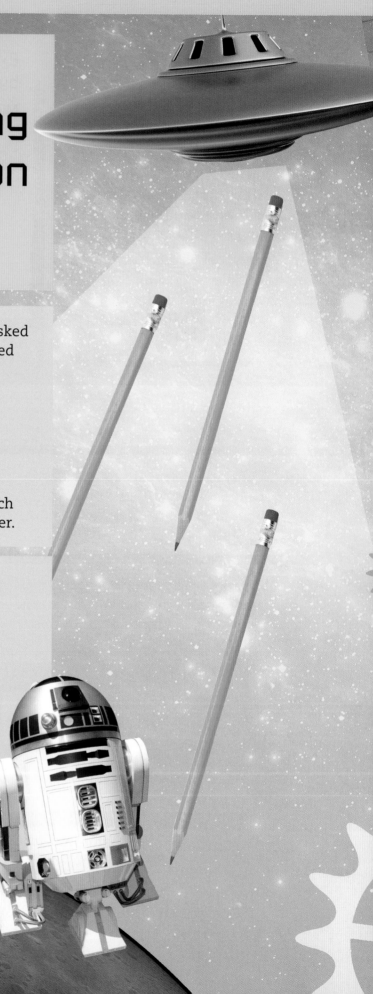

As part of a writing competition, you have been asked to write the opening of a science-fiction story based on one of the following:

- alien creatures

- robots

- space or time travel

- your own idea.

The winner will be asked to write a full story, which will be promoted by a new science-fiction publisher.

The judges will be looking for skill in:

- using features of science fiction to create an engaging opening for the reader

- using a range of sentence structures and vocabulary to create interest

- writing in accurate paragraphs and sentences with correct punctuation and spelling.

In particular, they will want to see:

- a consistent use of narrative voice

- powerful description

- creation of atmosphere and tension.

Before you write...

Planning: Use the knowledge and skills you have learned throughout this unit.

Think about how you are going to plan your opening, including:

- what makes a good story opening
- the atmosphere you want to create
- how you are going to hook your reader and keep their interest.

Also think about structure, organizing your ideas into paragraphs and choosing an effective opening sentence.

As you write...

Reviewing and editing: Check that you are following your plan, keeping your aims in mind and re-reading what you have written to make sure it makes sense and is creating the effect you want to achieve.

When you have finished writing...

Proofreading: Check that what you have written is clear and accurate, with correct punctuation and spelling. Particularly, check for errors that you know you tend to make in your writing.

4

Travellers' Tales

How does the power of language allow us to travel the world?

Introduction

Ever since the first cave people decided to explore the neighbouring valley and returned to tell their stories around the campfire, we have been enthralled by travellers' tales.

In this unit, you will travel in a taxi through a traffic jam in a busy Indian city, ride a camel across the Sahara, eat bugs in Bangkok and learn what it's like to suffer from altitude sickness on a train ride through the Andes, amongst other astonishing experiences. But how does the power of language allow us to travel the world without ever leaving our chairs?

ignite *INTERVIEW*
Hugh Thomson, Travel writer

Travel writing appeals to people partly because it is a way of escaping. You are going to a different part of the world and finding out what it is like. One important thing about travel writing is it doesn't have to be an exotic journey. You can write about any journey. It can be about your journey that is local, that is very close to you. It can be a journey that you have taken many times, so you know it really well. When you are choosing a story to write about, it should be a story that is important to you and at the heart of it should be something exciting.

✎ Activities

1a In pairs, describe a place you have visited. This could be somewhere local or a place you have visited on holiday.

1b As you listen to your partner, note down any effective words or phrases that they use which help to give you a sense of the place they are describing.

digital TV

1 First Impressions

↻ Objective

Identify and explore how a writer uses punctuation and vocabulary to create a sense of place.

Your first impression of a foreign country can be an overwhelming one. In the extract on page 89, the writer, Geoff Dyer, describes a hair-raising taxi ride experienced by a traveller on his arrival in the Indian city of Varanasi.

✎ Activities

1 How does the author's choice of vocabulary help to give you a sense of what the traffic is like in Varanasi? Think about: **SPAG**

- the choice of **verbs**, e.g. 'herded', 'roared'
- the **nouns** used, e.g. 'stampede'
- the contrasts and comparisons he makes, e.g. 'the full-metal frenzy of Saigon'.

2 The way the author uses punctuation also helps to create a sense of the situation. For example, using commas to pile up nouns in a sentence so that they resemble the traffic themselves: **SPAG**

'Cars, rickshaws, tuk-tuks, cars, bikes, carts, rickshaws, motorbikes, trucks, people, goats, cows, buffalo and buses were all herded together.'

Look at the following sentences and explain how punctuation is used in each one.

- 'The streets were narrow, potholed, trenched, gashed.'
- 'There was no pavement, no right of way – no wrong of way – and, naturally, no stopping.'
- 'Given the slightest chance – a yard! – Sanjay went for it.'

3 This scene is going to be filmed for a travel documentary. Create the voice-over for the scene. Remember to read with expression to convey a sense of rising panic.

Extract from *Death in Varanasi* by Geoff Dyer

'You need three things if you are driving in **Benares**,' he said; 'Good horn, good brakes and good luck.' He said it spontaneously, in an off-the-cuff style that had obviously been honed in the course of picking up hundreds of new arrivals.

'A seatbelt might be handy too,' I said. It was the last thing I said for some time because Sanjay, the driver, I realized now, had just been warming up, idling, girding his loins for what lay ahead. I am no stranger to the mighty traffics of Asia. I am a veteran of the perma-jams of Manila, the jihad of Java, the full-metal frenzy of Saigon, but this was something else. Cars, rickshaws, tuk-tuks, cars, bikes, carts, rickshaws, motorbikes, trucks, people, goats, cows, buffalo and buses were all herded together. The sheer quantity of traffic was the sole safeguard, the only thing that prevented a stampede. At one point we came to a roundabout and went round it, clockwise; others went round it anti-clockwise. Given the ability to do so, everyone would have done neither, would have just roared over it. The din of horns rendered use of the horn simultaneously **superfluous** and essential. The streets were narrow, potholed, trenched, gashed. There was no pavement, no right of way – no wrong of way – and, naturally, no stopping. The flow was so dense that we were rarely more than an inch from whatever was in front, beside or behind. But we never stopped. Not for a moment. We kept nudging and bustling and bumping our way forward. Given the slightest chance – a yard! – Sanjay went for it. What, in London, would have constituted a near-miss was an opportunity to acknowledge the courtesy of a fellow-road-user. There were no such opportunities, of course, and the idea of courtesy made no sense for the simple reason that nothing made any sense except the relentless need to keep going. From the airport to the hotel, Sanjay had used the horn excessively; now that we were in the city proper, instead of using it repeatedly, he kept it going all the time. So did everyone else. Unlike everything else, this did make sense. Why take your hand off the horn when, a split-second later, you'd have to put it back on?

📖 Glossary

verbs 'doing' or action words, e.g. *ran, laughed, screamed*

nouns words used to name people, places, things, ideas and animals, e.g. *Spain, dog, school*

Benares the old name for Varanasi

superfluous unnecessary

2 Expect the Unexpected

↻ Objectives

- Identify the ways in which a writer creates a tone that is appropriate for audience and purpose.

- Explore how travel writers use language to share their experiences.

Guidebooks and travel apps help travellers today learn more about the places they visit. However, sometimes they don't give a complete picture. Read the extract from a travel website about the city of Huancayo in Peru and then complete the activities on page 91.

📖 Glossary

Andean relating to the Andes – a mountain range in South America

altitude height above sea level

incomparable without equal in quality

Find Hotels | Book Flights

Extract from
Huancayo Travel Guide

If you're looking to take your travels off the beaten path, head up to Huancayo for a taste of authentic **Andean** culture. Huancayo is a city filled with history and tradition, known for its crafts, trekking and ruins. With more festivals than days of the year, you'll find something to do and see all year round.

Gallery 1 2 3 4 5 6

Overview

Huancayo is the capital […] of the Peruvian Central Andes sitting at around 10,650 feet in **altitude**. With an approximate population of 350,000, the city is nestled in the Mantaro Valley, surrounded by agricultural towns. You'll experience weather extremes in Huancayo – temperatures can range from 5 to 20 degrees throughout the day, there may be sudden thundershowers or hail (especially during the rainy season from October to April) and the sun burns, so be sure to wear sunscreen…

Getting to Huancayo

Although there is an airport […] around 50km away from the city, you would still need to take a 1 to 2-hour […] bus-ride to get from the local airport to Huancayo. It's easiest to take a 6 to 8-hour bus-ride directly from Lima east into the mountains […]

For those who have a little extra cash to spend, they say that the 12-hour tourist train-ride to Huancayo offers **incomparable** views through the Andes.

✎ Activities

1a Pick out the words and phrases that make Huancayo sound like an attractive place to visit.

1b Which details suggest that a visit to Huancayo might be challenging?

1c Discuss whether you would like to visit Huancayo after reading this guide.

SPAG

The tone of a text is the way in which it addresses its readers and its subject. In this text, the writer addresses the reader directly, using contractions to create a friendly and informal tone:

'If you're looking to take your travels off the beaten path...'

On pages 92–93, the writer, Paul Theroux, describes his train journey to Huancayo. As the journey progresses, he begins to experience the effects of high altitude.

2 Which of the following words would you choose to describe the tone of that extract and why?

friendly

emotional

fearful

calm

uneasy

enthusiastic

panicky

3a How does Paul Theroux help you to understand what it feels like to suffer from altitude sickness? Re-read the extract to identify the symptoms of altitude sickness.

▨ Support

Comment on the vocabulary the writer chooses to describe his symptoms, e.g. 'a sickening chill'.

3b Pick out a sentence that you think is especially effective in describing his experience. Explain why you have chosen it.

4 Write a new paragraph for the 'Getting to Huancayo' section on the travel website on page 90. This should advise travellers who are going to travel to Huancayo by train what might happen to them and the action they can take. Think about:

- the information you need to provide
- the tone you want to create.

☑ Progress Check

Swap your writing with a partner. How helpful is the advice they have provided? Can you suggest any ways to improve the tone of their writing?

More to explore

Extract from *The Old Patagonian Express: By Train Through the Americas* by Paul Theroux

It begins as dizziness and a slight headache. I had been standing by the door inhaling the cool air of these shady ledges. Feeling wobbly, I sat down, and if the train had not been full I would have lain across the seat. After an hour I was perspiring and, although I had not stirred from my seat, I was short of breath. The evaporation of this sweat in the dry air gave me a sickening chill. The other passengers were limp, their heads bobbed, no one spoke, no one ate. I dug some aspirin out of my suitcase and chewed them, but only felt queasier; and my headache did not **abate**. The worst thing about feeling so ill **in transit** is that you know that if something goes wrong with the train – a derailment or a crash – you will be too weak to save yourself. I had a more horrible thought: we were perhaps a third of the way to Huancayo, but Huancayo was higher than this. I dreaded to think what I would feel like at that altitude.

I considered getting off the train at Matucana, but there was nothing at Matucana – a few goats and some Indians and tin-roofed shacks on the stony ground. None of the stops contained anything that looked like relief or refuge. But this altitude sickness had another punishing aspect: it ruined what could have been a trip of astonishing beauty. I had never seen cliffs like these or been on a railway quite so spectacular… why was it, in this landscape of such unbelievable loveliness, that I felt as sick as a dog? If only I had the strength to concentrate – I would have been dazzled: but, as it was, the beauty became an extraordinary annoyance.

📖 Glossary

abate   get better

in transit   during a journey

The pale rose-coloured mountains had the dark stripes and mottled marks of the shells of the most delicate snails. To be ill among them, to be slumped in my seat watching the reddish gravel slides stilled in the crevasses, and the configuration of cliff-faces changing with each change in altitude, was torture so acute that I began to associate the very beautiful with the very painful. These pretty heights were the cause of my sickness. And now my teeth hurt, one molar in particular began to ache as if the nerve had caught fire. I did not know then how a cavity in a bad tooth becomes sore at a high altitude. The air in this blocked hole expands and creates pressure on the nerve, and it is agony. The dentist who told me this had been in the air force. Once, in a sharply descending plane, the cockpit became depressurised and an airman, the navigator, screamed in pain and then one of his teeth exploded.

Some of the train passengers had begun to vomit. They did it in the pitiful unembarrassed way that people do when they are helplessly ill. They puked on the floor, and they puked out of the windows and they made my own nausea greater. Some, I noticed, were staggering through the cars. I thought they were looking for a place to puke, but they returned with balloons. Balloons? Then they sat and held their noses and breathed the air from the balloon nozzle.

I stood unsteadily and made for the rear of the train, where I found a Peruvian in a smock filling balloons from a tank of oxygen. He handed these out to distressed-looking passengers who gratefully gulped from them. I took my place in the queue and discovered that a few whiffs of oxygen made my head clear and helped my breathing.

There was a boy in this oxygen car. He had an oxygen balloon, too, and wore a handsome cowboy hat decorated with a band of Inca poker-work.

'If I had thought it was going to be anything like this,' he said, 'I would never have come.'

'You took the words out of my mouth.'

🕐 Extra Time

Use the Internet to find articles from other travellers who have travelled by train in the Andes. How effectively have they described their experience?

3 Home Comforts

↺ Objective

Explore how noun phrases and other techniques are used to add descriptive detail.

'You have to edit your travel writing and go over it carefully – deciding what you keep in and what you leave out.'

Hugh Thomson

Most holidaymakers expect luxury from the hotels they stay in, but some intrepid travellers are looking for something a little different. Read the extract below from an online brochure advertising an unusual hostel in Sweden.

SWEDEN'S MOST PRIMITIVE HOTEL

Availability   Make a booking

At STF Kolarbyn neither electricity nor running water disturb your wilderness experience. Here you can happily fall asleep in front of the crackling fireplace and awake to beautiful bird song.

Silence, wilderness and exciting outdoor experiences are located just a few hours from intense big city life.

The hostel is a collection of twelve charcoal-burner huts located in the middle of a spruce forest. There are two bunks in each for sheepskins and sleeping bags. All the huts have a wood heated stove and use wood chopped by the guests themselves. Blueberries can be picked right off the roof of the hut.

Close by there are endless possibilities for enjoying outdoor life, including splendid fishing lakes, barbecues and hiking trails. The environmentally friendly hostel has been built

24 Comments (read more)   Rate it ★★★★★

from natural materials, and a percentage of the revenue coming into STF Kolarbyn goes straight to a range of projects that support preservation of the environment and historic places of interest. A visit to the hostel will be an exciting and enjoyable nature experience for young and old.

✏ Activities

1 Would you like to stay in this hostel? Discuss the positives and negatives of spending a week at STF Kolarbyn.

2 The advert uses expanded **noun phrases** to add detail to its description of the hostel. Here the **adjective** 'environmentally friendly' modifies the noun 'hostel', while the clause that follows adds additional information to the noun:

> 'The environmentally friendly hostel has been built from natural materials.'

How does the online brochure make the hostel sound appealing? Select details from the text and comment on their effectiveness.

SPAG

▧ Support

Look for examples of expanded noun phrases and use of the **rule of three**.

3 Imagine your own unusual hotel, for example, an underground cave or an ice hotel. Write an online brochure using expanded noun phrases and other techniques to make the hotel sound appealing.

↔ Stretch

Write an online review of your hotel from a family who are used to luxury accommodation. Think about how you could use modal verbs such as 'will', 'can', 'shall', 'may', 'could', 'should', 'would', 'might' and 'must' to help express views that are certain, probable or possible, e.g. 'We will *never* visit this hotel again.'

SPAG

📖 Glossary

noun phrase   a group of words built up around a single noun, e.g. *the very hungry snake*. The noun (snake in this example) is called the 'head' of the phrase because all the other words tell us something about the noun.

adjective   a word that describes a noun, e.g. *happy, blue, furious*

rule of three   grouping words and phrases in threes for added effect

4 Exotic Tastes

↺ Objectives

- Explore how a writer presents information appropriately for audience and purpose.

- Present information persuasively for listeners in a speech.

Even the most intrepid traveller can find themselves in need of advice. Read the extract from *Your Guide to Eating Insects in Bangkok* on page 97 and then complete the activities.

✎ Activities

1 What is your reaction to this text? Discuss what you think the purpose of the text is. Who is the audience for this guide?

2 The author uses a number of techniques to help the reader understand and enjoy the guide. These include writing in an informal style and using **rhetorical questions**. List examples of these from the text and any other techniques that you can spot that the writer uses to engage the reader.

SPAG

3 Re-read the guide to find the different words and phrases the writer uses to refer to insects, e.g. 'creepy-crawly things'.

Sort the list of words and phrases into positive and negative terms. Which are there more of and why do you think this is?

4 Write and present a speech for a school assembly persuading students to take part in an insect-eating challenge to raise money for school. Think about the ways you can present information about eating insects in a way that will encourage students to take part in the challenge.

◈ Support

You don't want to make the insects sound too revolting, so think about the words and phrases you could use to describe them. Ask rhetorical questions and use humour to entertain and amuse your audience.

☑ Progress Check

Give feedback on the speeches you have heard. Identify the techniques speakers used to keep your attention and suggest ways in which they could have improved their speech.

Your Guide to Eating Insects in Bangkok

As the saying goes, while in Rome, do as the Romans do, so while you're in Bangkok, you'll want to do as the Thai people do. This includes trying the food that makes Bangkok special. You might have to step out of your comfort zone if you really want to have the full experience.

What are your thoughts on insects? Those creepy-crawly things, usually the **recipient** of a well-placed shoe in other parts of the world, are quite the **commodity** in Bangkok for the Thai diet. These cringe-worthy creatures can be tasty and are actually very nutritious. Let's take a look at some of these scrumptious critters.

Where to find them

You'll have no trouble finding some fried delicacies at many of the push-carts on the streets of Bangkok. Khao San Road and Pat Pong are just two of the streets where you can find these rolling restaurants. How about trying some grasshoppers, crickets, or queen ants? You'll often find them deep-fried and served on a stick, while some are fried and then served in bags with a special, secret sauce. Sounds delightful, doesn't it?

If you're really determined to try some insects in Bangkok, Khao San Road is the place to start. You'll have no trouble finding a good variety to test your palate. Several night markets around

Bangkok also serve up insects, like Ratchadapisek Night Market on Saturdays and every night near the Major Ratchayothin Mall. Just take a walk around Bangkok and look for a push cart and you'll probably find some insects on the menu.

Even more unusual

Insects aren't the only thing being served up in Bangkok. Scorpions, members of the arachnid family, are harder to find. If you're "lucky" enough to find some, you better grab them up quickly, as they go fast. They are usually deep-fried and often served on a stick for easy consumption. Their exoskeleton makes eating them more challenging however.

Other popular delicacies are silk worms and bamboo worms. Technically, they're not insects, but they're just as disgusting, if not more so, for the insect-eating impaired. You'll want to know that they look crunchy, but they're not. It could be an unwelcome surprise to bite into a worm that is soft and mushy when you're expecting a crunchy texture. If you think you can handle it, then go for it. You might like them.

📖 Glossary

rhetorical question   a question asked for dramatic effect where the answer is not required

recipient   a person or thing that receives something

commodity   a useful or valuable thing

5 A Remote Meeting

↻ Objective

Retell a story from a different perspective, using voice and action to add impact.

When travellers venture into very remote regions, it is still possible for them to encounter communities who have never met outsiders before. In the extract on page 99, James Dorsey describes how he and his wife were treated by the inhabitants of a Maasai village in the Kenyan bush.

✎ Activities

1 Why are the villagers so fascinated by the nylon tent? Pick out three details from the text and explain how these show the villagers' fascination.

2 Discuss how the writer feels about the villagers. Do his feelings change at all in the passage?

3 How might one of the Maasai tell the story of the 'instant hut'? Think about:

- how the story would sound from the villagers' viewpoint
- which details might change and why
- the techniques they might use to interest their audience.

Working in the role of a Maasai villager, tell the story of the 'instant hut'.

📚 Support

Use the following techniques to keep your listeners' interest:

- Speak clearly and look directly at your audience.
- Vary the volume and tone of your voice for emphasis.
- Use actions and facial expressions to express feelings or for emphasis.
- Pause at key moments for effect.

↔ Stretch

Improvise a conversation between James or Irene and one of the villagers. What would they want to say even though they can't understand each other?

EXTRACT FROM *THE WARRIOR SCHOLAR FROM KENYA* BY JAMES DORSEY

No sooner were Irene and I inside the tent than most of the village had surrounded us, pulling the zipper up and down while running their hands over the strange new sensation of nylon. Most of them had never seen a tent before, and called it an "instant hut".

A full moon was rising over the tree line, and it turned the silhouettes of our curious visitors into an ongoing puppet show crawling over our tent walls as they continued to play with the zipper and occasionally thrust an ebony head inside to giggle at us strange creatures.

Surreal patterns glided over the tent wall as tiny fingers and old hands ran up and down. We were as much an oddity as a circus act and at first we stayed inside, hoping to minimize our impact, but this only fed the people's curiosity as more and more poked their heads inside for a brief glimpse of us.

This went on until I stepped outside to see just how many people there were who had yet to pay us a visit.

To my surprise, a line of people snaked through the forest and down into the valley where word had spread about these visitors and their instant hut, and now the entire valley was migrating towards our tent. As far as I could see, Maasai were coming from all around to see us.

Irene stepped outside to greet our visitors. Most shook our hands while others simply wanted to touch us. For some, we would be the only white people they would ever know. No one spoke and there was no need for words. In that magical evening we were all simply people, coming together to meet each other for the first and only time, frozen by a human touch that instantly passed into memory.

I stepped back inside the tent, laying next to Irene and watched this never ending procession of shadows through the night. There would be no sleep and we did not care. No festival, ceremony, or dance could have been more entertaining or enlightening to us. The Maasai are story tellers, and in Africa, especially among tribes with no written language, stories quickly become both history and legend. Stories tend to grow with each telling and take on the flavour of the narrator. I know that evening we became a story to be told around their campfires for generations to come.

Comments   Submit

⏰ **Extra Time**

Some people think that remote societies should be left alone because contact with the outside world is likely to harm them. Decide whether you agree or disagree and find evidence to support your point of view.

6 A Scary Moment

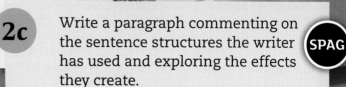

↻ Objective

Explore how writers shape and craft sentences to create mood and meaning, and use these techniques in your own writing.

Writers use a variety of sentence structures to create different effects – for example, using longer, complex sentences to describe several things happening at the same time or using short sentences for dramatic impact. In the travel article on page 101, Mandy Huggins and her friend Marnie decide to venture on to the sands of the Sahara for the first time.

✎ Activities

1 Summarize the events of the article in 20 words or fewer.

2a The **mood** of the passage changes dramatically as the events unfold. Create a flow diagram identifying the mood created in each paragraph.

2b For each paragraph, select a quotation that helps to create the mood. This might be a word, phrase or sentence.

2c Write a paragraph commenting on the sentence structures the writer has used and exploring the effects they create. **SPAG**

3 Write a description of a visit to a place where the mood changes as events unfold. This could be based on your own experience or you could use one of the following ideas:

- A bike ride into the countryside goes wrong.
- A trip into town turns into a nightmare.
- A family outing turns into a disaster.

Think about the sentence structures and vocabulary you can use to signal the mood.

📖 Glossary

mood   the emotions conveyed to a reader in a piece of writing

☑ Progress Check

Annotate your description to highlight some of the different sentence structures you have used. Comment on the effects you wanted the sentences to create. **SPAG**

EXTRACT FROM

TALES FROM THE EDGE OF THE SAHARA BY MANDY HUGGINS

The next morning we rush headlong to the edge of the desert, feeling the sand rush softly between our fingers, scooping it into a tiny bottle that once held fig liquor. We climb to the top of a dune, laughing and sliding, wrapping our blue berber scarves around our faces. A boy in a neon shell suit introduces himself as Ali, and points to his two camels, Pauli and Pipa. Powerless to resist Pipa's sweeping eyelashes, we agree a price for a two-hour trek.

We stroll out into the desert, silenced by the clarity of the light and the depth of the shadows. Eventually Douz disappears from sight, and we lose all sense of direction. Marnie asks Ali if we can go faster. He lets go of Pipa for a moment as he starts to run with Pauli's rope, giving him a quick thwack with his stick for good measure. The camel expresses his dismay with a loud bellow, and as he digs his heels in, Pipa takes the cue to set off at full tilt.

At first I am in shock. I hold on tightly to the pommel as Pipa gallops into eternity, heading further and further into the dunes. I shout at her in vain as my scarf unwraps itself and floats upwards like a distress flare.

Then I panic. I am scarcely managing to hold on, and we are still accelerating. I resort to drastic action, and jump. I land awkwardly, winded, on what feels like concrete. Pipa keeps right on galloping without missing a beat.

With nothing except sky and dunes […] as far as the eye can see, it seems impossible that I will find my way back without a camel, a compass or water. The thought of water brings with it an instant raging thirst, and in no time at all I am hallucinating.

There is a mirage on the horizon; the tiny neon-pink figure of Ali, running towards me, waving his arms. Marnie follows, leading Pauli.

It turns out Pipa was following the trekking route back to the other camels and I wasn't really lost. "Good fast camel, non?" beams Ali as he helps me to my feet. Needless to say, he doesn't get a tip.

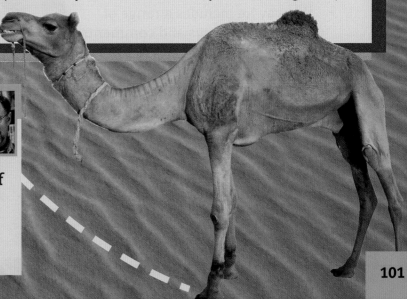

ignite INTERVIEW

'What really matters to me is that at the heart of my writing there is something exciting, because if it doesn't excite me, it is certainly not going to excite any reader.'

Hugh Thomson

7 Tall Tales

↻ Objectives

- Explore how writers create convincing descriptions.

- Participate in a discussion, presenting your own views and building on others'.

The best travel writers make their readers feel as though they have visited the places they describe through the power of their writing. But how can we really know that what they write is true? The extract on page 103 is taken from *The Travels of Sir John Mandeville*, a bestselling book published in the 14th century, which claimed to describe the amazing sights the author had seen during his lifetime of travelling.

✎ Activities

1 Explore the way that Sir John Mandeville makes his writing so convincing. Discuss:

- the descriptive and geographical details he includes

- the way he includes a range of names with views and comments

- how he appeals to the senses of hearing, sight and smell.

It has since been discovered that Sir John Mandeville was unlikely to have been a real person and most of the travels described in his book were in fact invented or based on other writers' accounts.

2 Does this change your opinion about the text you have just read? Re-read the extract to identify clues that suggest to you this description was invented.

3 Nowadays, do writers even need to visit the places they write about? Discuss the following statements:

> The Internet allows you to see the world without even leaving your house.

> You can't really understand another country unless you have visited it.

> Travel broadens the mind.

> Being a tourist doesn't really allow you to experience a country.

Remember to present your own point of view and build on what others say.

▤ Support

Listen carefully to others and think about whether you agree or disagree with the points that they make. You could:

- support their viewpoint, giving reasons why you agree

- challenge their point of view, explaining why you disagree

- question their viewpoint, asking for evidence to support what they say.

4 Write a description of an invented place such as 'The Mountain of Solitude' or 'The Valley of Screams'.

↔ Stretch

Try to write your description in the style of Sir John Mandeville. Look at the sentence structures and other features of his writing and use these in your own writing for a Fantastical Travel website.

📖 Glossary

perilous full of danger

tempests storms

tabor a type of drum

heathen a person who does not belong to a religion

covetousness desire for wealth

Extract from *The Travels of Sir John Mandeville* by Sir John Mandeville

A little way from that place towards the River Phison [Ganges] is a great marvel. For there is a valley between two hills, about four miles long; some men call it the Vale of Enchantment, some the Vale of Devils, and some the Vale **Perilous**.

In this valley there are often heard **tempests**, and ugly, hideous noises, both by day and by night. And sometimes noises are heard as if of trumpets and **tabors** and drums, like at the feasts of great lords. This valley is full of devils and always has been, and men of those parts say it is an entrance to Hell. There is much gold and silver in this valley, and to get it many men – Christian and **heathen** – come and go into that valley. But very few come out again – least of all unbelievers – for all who go therein out of **covetousness** are strangled by devils and lost. In the middle of the valley under a rock one can clearly see the head and face of a devil, very hideous and dreadful to see; nothing else is seen of it except from the shoulders up. There is no man in this world, Christian or anyone else, who would not be very terrified to see it, it is so horrible and foul. He looks at each man so keenly and so cruelly, and his eyes are rolling so fast and sparkling like fire, and he changes his expression so often, and out of his nose and mouth comes so much fire of different colours with such an awful stench, that no man can bear it.

8 Assessment: Writing the Script for a Podcast Designed for Young People

Plan, write and create.

The Ends of The Earth is a very popular travel website which attracts a huge adult readership. We feel that now is the time for us to reach a new audience – young people between the ages of 10 and 14 – and we need your help.

As part of our plans for expansion, we want to offer young people the opportunity to contribute to a new section of the website entitled 'A Fresh View'. This will contain a range of content, all written by young people for young people. It will present a new, fresh approach to travel and we would like you to be one of our launch contributors.

Please create a podcast of no more than four minutes on one of the following subjects:

- A journey I have taken – a description of your experience
- My home town – an informative and engaging guide for visitors
- A place I would love to visit – a description of the place and why it appeals to you.

We look forward to listening to your podcast. If the new section of the site is successful, we hope that you will become a regular contributor.

Planning your podcast...

When writing your podcast you should:

- appeal to a young audience
- be as descriptive or informative as possible
- follow a clear structure with a beginning, middle and end.

Creating your podcast...

Remember that your podcast will be sound only, so your language will have to be clear, precise and descriptive.

- Use **Standard English** unless **dialect** is used for effect.
- Speak clearly and at a controlled pace.
- Use expression in your voice.
- Address your audience.

Note that, for the purposes of this assessment, you will be marked on your writing and speaking skills.

📖 Glossary

Standard English   the variety of English that is regarded as 'correct' and is used in more formal situations. It is not specific to any geographical area and can be spoken or written.

dialect   informal words used in a specific geographical area

5

MAKING THE NEWS

HOW DOES THE NEWS MAKE IT TO THE BIG SCREEN?

Introduction

Want to keep millions informed about what's happening in the world? Bring the news to people's front rooms the moment that it happens? Change people's minds while they're sitting on their sofas? Working in TV news can give you the chance to do all these things.

In this unit, you will find out what it is really like working for a TV production company and have the chance to plan, draft and present a report for a TV news bulletin. Get ready to take a look behind the credits and find out what it takes to get the news onscreen.

ignite INTERVIEW
Will Gompertz, BBC Arts Correspondent

The trick of really good broadcast television, or public speaking in any format, is to realize how powerful your character is in front of the people to whom you are performing. Energy, commitment and warmth are the crucial assets of any presenter, whether you are doing it on television or in the classroom. Perhaps the most important thing that one has to realize about the news business is that you are in the story-telling business. You have got to make it exciting for the person who is going to watch it. That means you have to think about the words that you choose, the structure of your narrative and the way that you want to reveal the story.

Activities

1 Discuss what you think people in each of the following jobs in TV do. If you're not sure, think about the clues the job title gives you. The first one has been done for you.

- Runner: a person who runs errands on a TV shoot (for example, delivering messages, organizing props, etc)
- Researcher
- Scriptwriter
- Editor
- Director

2 Which one of the jobs appeals to you most? Why?

ON AIR

1 Who Makes the News?

↻ Objective

Understand the roles involved in TV news production and the skills required for these.

There are two main types of TV news programmes:

- National news, which presents news stories of national and international importance, e.g. major crimes, disasters, sports, the arts, etc.

- Regional news, which presents news stories that are of importance to a specific area, e.g. a county such as Greater London or geographical region such as north-west England.

You can split people who work in TV news into two teams:

- News gatherers: people who gather information about different news stories.

- News producers: people who use the material collected to create the TV news **bulletin**.

📖 Glossary

bulletin   a short news programme

NEWS GATHERERS

NEWS PRODUCERS

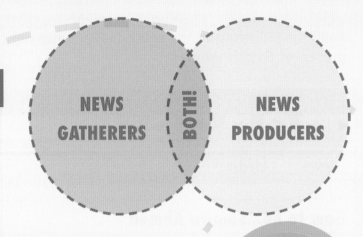

NEWS GATHERERS   BOTH!   NEWS PRODUCERS

✎. Activities

1 Look at the following roles in TV news and identify which team you think each one belongs to. You might want to put some roles in more than one team (news gatherers and news producers).

A camera person shoots film to record a news story in a clear and interesting way. They might also edit the film to create the clip you see on the TV news.

A reporter investigates news stories. They will go out of the studio to report on them, but might also speak live to the presenter back in the studio.

The producer decides on the running order of the news bulletin: for example, which news stories are included, what order they are shown in and how they are presented onscreen.

The director is in charge of the news bulletin while it is being broadcast. They will speak to other members of the news team, such as the presenter, to make sure the programme runs smoothly.

The presenter anchors the news bulletin and speaks directly to the viewer. They read from a script to present each news story, but might also interview reporters or other guests.

↔ Stretch

Can you think of any other roles in a TV news team? Describe these and, for each one, decide whether it is a 'news gatherer' or 'news producer' job.

More to explore

Read the following article about the TV news reporter and presenter, Samira Ahmed.

News   Media

How to be...Samira Ahmed

Television has been part of my life since I was just eight years old. *Newsround* aired an item I sent them about being attacked in a racist incident at my school playground. I had previously **harboured** ambitions in **print journalism**, but my *Newsround* debut gave me the hunger to work in television.

I combined my degree with editing a student publication and went on to study newspaper journalism in London. Despite this experience, I went for a place on the BBC news trainee scheme and it changed my life. I realised I loved writing for TV and radio during the two years I spent on **attachments** with different BBC outlets. My first proper job was as a radio network reporter. One of my most memorable days was the large march following the government announcement of the closure of 92 coalmines. Hundreds of thousands of people came to London from around Britain and it was a remarkable story to cover, with sound effects and celebrity interviews.

I never planned to be a newsreader, but Paul Gibbs at BBC *Breakfast News* gave me the chance while I was on attachment there and I discovered I was a natural. For nine months, aged 23, I presented news to millions around the world, notably the storming of the Russian White House.

When I left university, the Berlin Wall was coming down. Since then there has been a whole set of meaty issues for journalists to get their teeth into. If you have got a reporter's instinct it just does not die; I am still genuinely interested in getting answers out of people.

Career high   Moving to C4 News. I have been able to do more in-depth reporting and pursue my own obsessions.

Career low   I was 24 and couldn't cope with the unexpected when I was sent to cover a suspected bomb in Whitehall. I lost the radio car, but when I found it, I panicked while **adlibbing** for the midnight bulletin. The whole of BBC news could hear me messing up live on location and I thought my career was over.

📖 Glossary

harboured   had secret

print journalism   newspapers

attachments   work experience

adlibbing   speaking without a script

✎ Activities continued

2 What first interested Samira Ahmed in working in TV news?

3 What skills and experiences do you think Samira Ahmed has needed as a TV news reporter and presenter? Try to find evidence from the article to support your suggestions.

📚 Support

Look at the section headed 'Career low'. What skills do you think Samira Ahmed needed in that situation?

↔ Stretch

What do you think a 'reporter's instinct' is? Write a short explanation.

4 Role-play an interview for the job of a TV news reporter. Discuss the questions that could be asked and take it in turns to be the interviewer.

☑ Progress Check

Identify three skills that you have that would make you a good TV news reporter. For each one, give an example of a time when you have shown this skill.

ignite INTERVIEW

'Broadcast journalism is a team effort and it is absolutely crucial that you work as a team, that you listen to each other and you support each other. Everybody can make a contribution.'

Will Gompertz

2 Choosing the News

↻ Objectives

- Understand the structure and features of a TV news bulletin.

- Evaluate the importance of different news stories to a specific audience, making clear and relevant contributions to a discussion.

TV news bulletins usually follow the same format:

- **Opening segment:** The presenter introduces the top news stories coming up in the bulletin.

- **Lead story:** The most important story in the news that day. This might be told using a **video package**, **live action report**, interviews or **talking heads**.

- **Other news stories:** These are presented in order of importance.

- **'And finally':** A funny or light-hearted news story to end the bulletin.

📖 Glossary

video package reporter speaking over the top of different shots edited together

live action report reporter speaking live from the scene of the story

talking heads news presenter or reporter speaking directly to the camera

✎ Activities

1 News Report is a TV news bulletin that is broadcast at 5pm every night and is popular with a teenage audience. You have received the following email from the producer of News Report.

To: News Reporter

From: News Editor

Dear News Reporter

We have four different news stories for tonight's bulletin, but only have time to include three of these. I need your help to select the running order for the programme.

Read the summaries of the four different news stories on the opposite page. Discuss the merits of each story and decide which one should be dropped.

ignite INTERVIEW

'If you are presenting news on the television you are in the story-telling business. These are stories. That is what we call them. "What is your story? What story are we going to lead the news with today?" You have to make that bit of information that you have got live. You have got to make it exciting.'

Will Gompertz

STORY A: A school student has woken up paralysed. A 14-year-old schoolboy is recovering in hospital after going to bed with a cold and waking up paralysed. David Ramsden, a student at Newtown Comprehensive School in Manchester, was diagnosed with the rare Guillain-Barré syndrome, which causes the arms and legs to stop working.

STORY B: The price of haircuts has been ruled illegal. Hairdressers have warned of 'pricing chaos' after the Equal Opportunities Board ruled that charging different prices for men's and women's haircuts was illegal. 'It takes, quite simply, longer to cut women's hair,' said Sidney Siskin, who represents the Hairdressers and Beauticians Association.

STORY C: Residents evacuated 500 homes in St Asaph in north Wales after a river broke through flood defences. One elderly man had to be rescued from his home by fire and rescue crews. Householders have already evacuated 900 properties after heavy downpours left many homes uninhabitable, and caused road and rail chaos. With rising groundwater levels and river levels set to peak over the next 48 hours, forecasters have warned of more flooding.

STORY D: Australia is preparing for days of devastating fire and horrific heatwave conditions. Fires are already burning in five states and a search mission continues in Tasmania following catastrophic wildfires. On a tour of fire-damaged Tasmanian townships, the Australian Prime Minister promised emergency aid for survivors. Local residents spoke of a giant 'fireball' that destroyed regions of the island on Friday and Saturday.

2 Use the following criteria to assess the newsworthiness of each story:

- Is the news new? Has the story just happened?

- Is the news about people who the audience would be interested in?

- Is the news dramatic? Does the story involve conflict, catastrophe or other dramatic events?

- Is the news important? Does the story affect people in a certain area, across the country or around the world?

3 Decide on the running order for tonight's bulletin. Rank the three stories in order of importance.

4 Write an email to the producer giving your suggestions for the running order for tonight's news bulletin. Remember to explain:

- which story you have chosen as the lead story and why

- which story you have decided to drop and why.

⏱ Extra Time

Watch a TV news bulletin and note down the running order. Do you agree with the order the stories were presented in?

3 Explaining the Issues

↻ Objective

Understand some of the language and grammatical features used to convey information clearly and concisely in a TV news bulletin.

TV news bulletins often have to present and explain complex issues and ideas in a way that ordinary viewers will understand. Using simpler language and constructing sentences in ways that make information clear can help to do this.

Read the following introduction to a TV news report about a schoolboy who has been diagnosed with Guillain-Barré **syndrome**.

A 14-year-old schoolboy from Manchester has been left frozen in his own body by a freak medical condition. David Ramsden, a student at Newtown Comprehensive School, has been diagnosed by doctors as suffering from Guillain-Barré syndrome. This rare disease, which affects only one in 50,000 people in the UK, causes the body's **immune system** to attack part of the **nervous system**. Starting as a sensation of pins and needles, the disease can cause a person's arms and legs to stop working entirely. In some severe cases, such as David's, sufferers are left completely paralysed. There is hope for David though, as 80% of patients diagnosed with Guillain-Barré syndrome go on to make full recoveries.

✎ Activities

1 Re-read the first sentence of the news report. Does this give you the main point of the news story? Are there any other details you think should have been included here? Discuss your ideas.

2 How does the vocabulary used in the report help you to understand what Guillain-Barré syndrome is?

◈ Support

Look at how the effects of Guillain-Barré syndrome are described in the report:

- 'frozen in his own body'
- 'causes arms and legs to stop working entirely'
- 'completely paralysed'.

Why might the writer have chosen to describe the same symptom in three different ways?

3 Pick out the statistics included in the report and explain how these help the viewer to understand more about the disease.

↔ Stretch

Why do you think the writer has used statistics in the introduction to this report? Does the use of statistics make you more or less likely to believe what the presenter is telling you? Give reasons for your answer.

4 Re-read the following sentence from the report:

'This rare disease, which affects only one in 50,000 people in the UK, causes the body's immune system to attack part of the nervous system.'

Here the writer uses a **relative clause** to present additional information about the disease.

Pick out other examples of where clauses are used to present additional or clarifying information.

5 Remind yourself of the stories you selected for tonight's News Report bulletin (Activity 3, page 113). Draft an introduction to another of these stories, conveying the key information clearly and concisely.

SPAG

📖 Glossary

syndrome   a type of disease

immune system   the parts of your body that work together to fight disease

nervous system   the parts of your body that control your movement, e.g. brain, spinal cord, nerves, etc.

relative clause   a clause that modifies a noun or noun phrase and is introduced by a relative pronoun (e.g. 'which', 'that', 'who', 'whom', 'whose') or relative adverb (e.g. 'where', 'when', 'why')

4 Picture Power

↺ Objective

Explore how choices of image can indicate viewpoint and communicate information in a TV news report.

You have received another email from the producer of News Report.

To: News Reporter

From: News Editor

Dear News Reporter

This story about the Australian bush fires has got me thinking: We should link this report to the wider impact of **global warming** and invite two scientists on to the programme to debate the issues. Select an image that shows the threat of climate change – we will **superimpose** this on to the studio background during the interview.

✎ Activities

1 Which of the following images on the right would you choose? Discuss the reasons for your choice.

One of the scientists invited to discuss global warming on tonight's News Report is a **climate change sceptic**. She has complained that the image you have chosen is **biased** in favour of people who believe in climate change.

2 Why might the climate change sceptic think your selected image is biased? Discuss your ideas.

3 A researcher on the news team has sent you the picture on the right from a breaking news story. What do you think has happened?

Discuss what parts of the photograph gave you clues to work out what had happened. For example: *'One of the men is wearing a helmet and camouflage uniform, which suggests he is a soldier.'*

4a Think again about the stories you selected for tonight's News Report bulletin (Activity 3, page 113).

Choose one of the stories and decide on five images you want the camera person to film for the story.

4b Explain what viewpoint of the story you want to present with your choice of images.

☑ Progress Check

How confident are you about 'reading' an image? For example, do you know what the image does and does not tell us? Give yourself a rating from 1 to 10.

📖 Glossary

global warming the increasing temperature of the Earth's atmosphere

superimpose to place on top of

climate change sceptic somebody who doesn't believe in global warming

biased favouring one side over another

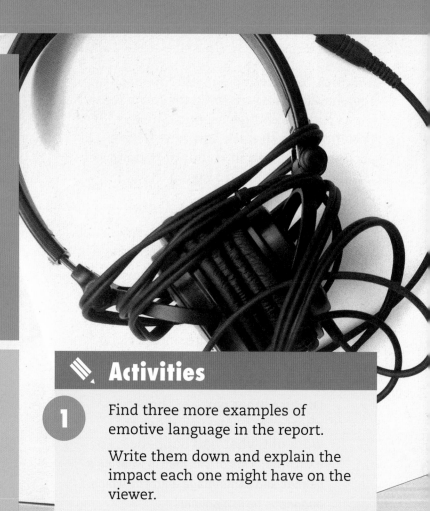

5 The Language of News

↻ Objective

Identify how language choices can indicate **bias**.

News reports sometimes try to influence viewers by using **emotive language**. For example, in the script for the news report about the bush fires in Australia below, the fires are described as 'horrific' and 'catastrophic'. The use of these strong **adjectives** makes us feel that they are really terrible events.

As hundreds of horrific bush fires sweep across south-east Australia, forecasters warn there is no end in sight for the scorching heatwave that has caused them. Soaring temperatures are predicted to continue over the weekend, fanning the flames of yet more wildfires. Government scientists have blamed the record-breaking heatwave on the impact of global warming, and warn that there is an increased likelihood that such catastrophic bush fires will occur more frequently in the future.

✎ Activities

1 Find three more examples of emotive language in the report.

Write them down and explain the impact each one might have on the viewer.

2 Rewrite the script by changing the adjectives used. Try to make the story sound less dramatic. **SPAG**

The producer has sent you the first draft of the script for a news item on the cost of haircuts. There are a lot of changes needed and the producer wants you to make them.

This script is far too biased! It needs to be more objective.

The cost of getting your hair cut is under attack from political correctness gone mad! The Equal Opportunities Board has ruled that charging different prices for men's and women's haircuts is illegal. There have been warnings of 'pricing chaos' and this crazy decision could result in huge increases to the cost of a short back and sides for the average man in the street. Sidney Siskin of the Hairdressers and Beauticians Association said "It takes, quite simply, longer to cut women's hair. How on earth can I justify charging the same to some bald bloke who just comes in for a trim?" This ridiculous ruling needs to be snipped in the bud and leave hairdressers free to charge fair prices.

Opening statement sounds very alarmist

Seems too emotive

Whose view is this? Need to present the counter-arguments too...

Needs to be more balanced

3 Rewrite the script so that it presents a more balanced view of the news story. Discuss what the positive effects of this change might be.

Remember, you aren't presenting your own point of view but providing the views on both sides of the argument in a balanced way. For example, you could add information to make it clear who holds a certain viewpoint: *'A spokesperson for the Hairdressers and Beauticians Association has claimed that the decision will lead to pricing chaos, but a recent survey of Mumsnet users showed that many women believe it will lead to fairer prices.'*

↔ Stretch

Try to provide evidence to support the arguments and counter-arguments you include in the report.

📖 Glossary

bias only presenting one viewpoint

emotive language words used to create an emotional response

adjective a word that describes a noun, e.g. *happy, blue, furious*

6 News in Vision

↻ Objective

Use role-play to explore different techniques for communicating information in a TV news scenario.

Approximately 80% of the information the average person's brain receives comes directly from their eyes. In order to communicate information clearly and effectively, TV news bulletins use a range of techniques to help tell the news in an interesting and stimulating way.

A director's choice of technique can depend on what the news story is about and who is available to help tell it.

- Talking head: The head of the news presenter, news reporter or interviewee is seen in one shot where they talk to the camera.

- Live action report: The reporter broadcasts live, standing in front of the camera with the scene behind them clearly visible.

- Interviews: These might take place in the studio, on location, or even 'down the line' where the news presenter in the studio interviews someone in a different location.

Activities

1 Look at page 113 to remind yourself of the stories that could be included in tonight's episode of News Report. Working as a group, choose one of the stories and use role-play to try out different ways of presenting this on screen.

Support

Think about the following:

- Would a live action report help to tell any of these news stories? Can you get a news reporter to the scene in time for tonight's News Report bulletin?

- Who might be interviewed to help explain the story to the viewer? Would this interview happen in the studio or on location?

Remember, you can use more than one technique to bring the story to the screen.

2 Re-read the script for the news story about the Australian bush fires at the top of the next column.

Copy and complete the following table to record the images and techniques you would choose to accompany each sentence in the script.

As hundreds of horrific bush fires sweep across south-east Australia, forecasters warn there is no end in sight for the scorching heatwave that has caused them. Soaring temperatures are predicted to continue over the weekend, fanning the flames of yet more wildfires. Government scientists have blamed the record-breaking heatwave on the impact of global warming, and warn that there is an increased likelihood that such catastrophic bush fires will occur more frequently in the future.

ignite INTERVIEW

'You as a journalist on television are not as important as the pictures or the sound or the guests, but the story is and you have got to put it across in a really precise way.'

Will Gompertz

Script	Images and techniques
'As hundreds of horrific bush fires sweep across south-east Australia, forecasters warn there is no end in sight...'	Talking head of news reporter live on location with backdrop of bush fire in shot

7 Reading the News

↻ Objective

Read a news script aloud, speaking clearly and fluently with appropriate pace, volume and action in a TV news scenario.

When reading a script, a news reporter needs to think about:

- the pace they read at
- their **intonation**
- their **tone of voice**
- where they look.

📖 Glossary

intonation   the rise and fall of a person's voice when they speak

tone of voice   the way words are spoken, e.g. a serious tone, a light-hearted tone, etc.

✎ Activities

1. Working in a group, practise reading this script aloud. Use the following tips to help you rehearse the script:

- Look at what the images show and think about the tone of voice you should use when reading the script.

- Identify the key information in the script. Think about how you can use the intonation of your voice to emphasize the most important information.

- Take your time – don't let your nerves make you rush your delivery of the script.

- If you make a mistake, don't worry – just correct yourself and carry on.

📑 Support

Think about the clues the punctuation gives you about the pace you should read at. The more times you rehearse, the more confident you'll be about what you are going to say.

Remember, you can use more than one technique to bring the story to the screen.

🕐 Extra Time

Watch one of the evening news bulletins from any TV channel. How many different tones of voice do you notice being used during the programme?

Script	Images
Jonathan Rugman voice-over:	A series of shots showing the scale of devastation in Waveland.
'It's the dawn of a new day in Waveland—once a seaside town of 7000 people—now flattened, ripped to shreds, wiped off the map…	A shot of collapsed houses at dawn.
… entire avenues reduced to rubble…	A view up a road—collapsed houses on both sides—the road curiously clear.
… at least 50 dead here—some of them found clinging for safety to the branches of trees…	A travelling shot taken from a vehicle showing more destruction beside the road.
… a few hungry pets now searching for owners who have fled.'	A view up the road showing a group of dogs barking amid the wreckage.
Brian Mollere: 'Beautiful morning!'	Interview with Brian Mollere—Waveland resident in the wreckage of his home.
Rugman voice-over:	Medium shot of Mollere.
'But Brian Mollere is staying put…	Close-up of his feet and a broom—as he sweeps his concrete floor.
… keeping as tidy as he can what's left of his home…	
Brian's mother died in the storm…	Long shot of tattered blue canopy surrounded by wreckage.
His dog, Rocky, didn't.'	Long shot of a tattered, unfurled Stars and Stripes flag.
Mollere: 'He held on to me like this. Rocky was on my arm as we swum out—he couldn't swim, his legs are too short. He made it—through the whole ordeal. Rocky say "hello".'	Mollere holds Rocky up to his shoulder.
Mollere: 'Getting ready to make some more coffee here…'	Close-up of Mollere heating water on a camping hob.
Rugman voice-over:	Shot of shelves containing groceries.
'Christian groups have given Brian food and he now camps beneath the stars—still marvelling at how he survived a surge of ocean water 25 feet high.'	Shot of SUV buried in rubble and mud.
Mollere: 'I think I survived. I was above this—up to the top of that pole—I would say 25 feet.'	Mollere in close-up—pointing to a point in mid-air.
Unseen interviewer: 'What were you doing up there?'	Shot from Mollere's point of top of canopy.

More to explore

Script	Images
'I was swimming—I had my little dog under my arm and I'm paddling with the other—going with the current. Trying to stay away from debris and houses and whatever was piled up…'	Mollere in close-up.
Rugman voice-over: 'Brian shares a gun with a friend to protect themselves from looters…' Friend: 'He protects himself with that…' Rugman voice over: 'Brian had no property insurance—his family couldn't afford it. But, he's still house proud and up-beat.'	Close-up of rifle being loaded. Shot of Mollere's 'friend' with rifle. Long shot of further devastation—Mollere's home in ruins.
Question: 'You're sweeping the floor today. Why are you doing that when you haven't got any walls?' Mollere: 'Well—this is home. We like to keep it nice and clean. This is where we live right now—nowhere else to go. We have company come by all the time so we like to keep it presentable.'	Shots of Mollere sweeping, then combination of close-up shots of Mollere and long shot views of him clearly out in the open.
Rugman voice-over: 'One mile back and Brian's former neighbours have pitched their tents in the car park of a shopping mall—picking through Salvation Army boxes for clothes that might fit… Three months ago, these soldiers were driving convoys across Iraq—now they are forming an outdoor supermarket checkout—the food free and donated by Walmart—every day the feeding of at least 3000.'	Establishing shots of tents. A series of long shots of soldiers distributing food and unloading supplies from a vehicle.

Script	Images
Rugman voice-over: 'And this is the local chemist—a medicine man so vital here that he and his drugs have to be protected from desperate looters.' Question: 'What kind of medical problems have you encountered?' Answer: 'Most people lost all their medicine. If you look over at the store, we had over 15 feet of water here and so anyone who lived from here towards the Gulf, their homes were completely underwater, destroyed. So they have no medicine for their heart, blood pressure, diabetes…'	Close-up of man in tent interior—baseball cap and dark glasses. He is giving advice about injections. Close-up of him writing prescriptions (scripts in US English). A low angle shot of him taken to include the camouflage trousers of a soldier and a rifle butt.
Rugman voice-over: 'But shortage of medicine isn't Susan St Amant's priority—it's how to fit her family of six inside this tent with another four relatives arriving tonight.'	A curious shot showing a shadow on a tent. Then a slow pan across the chaotic interior of the tent.
Susan St Amant: 'It's hard—I thought I had it hard before raising three kids by myself, but it's harder now, because they don't understand what's going on, they don't understand we have nothing.' Question: 'How are you going to pick your life up again—you've got no job, no house? You're living in a tent.' Susan St Amant: 'I don't know… I don't know…'	Close-up of Susan St Amant. A shot of the tent exterior and of groceries and possessions piled up in a supermarket trolley. Close-up of Susan St Amant weeping.
Rugman voice-over: 'And so this is life in all its grim reality in Waveland… … a town so devastated that even its railway tracks don't know where they're going.'	Exterior long shot of blonde child in nappies wandering around the car park in between the piles of groceries and possessions. Long shot of damaged railway lines.

8 Writing the News

Objective

Revise the techniques used to summarize information clearly and concisely.

At a meeting to discuss the final running order of tonight's edition of News Report, the producer drops a bombshell:

To: News Reporter

From: News Editor

Dear News Reporter

The 'And finally' story we originally picked isn't working. We need a new funny story fast. I've found this newspaper article and I think it's the perfect story to end tonight's bulletin. I want you to write me a script for a 60-second news report about this.

 Activities

1 Read the newspaper article on page 127. Then write the script that the presenter will use to introduce the story. This should last no longer than 15 seconds – approximately 40 words. Think about how you could:

- create a short, snappy opening to introduce the story

- choose vocabulary to present information entertainingly

- use punctuation to show how the script should be read aloud.

Support

You could use the following sentence to start your script:

Forget about 'Angry Birds', a pair of penguins in a Californian zoo have discovered their own favourite iPad game…

2 Make a list of the video pictures you want the camera person to film on location at the zoo. For example, '*a close-up of a penguin's beak tapping the iPad…*'

3 Write a voice-over from the news reporter to accompany the video package. You could include comments from an interview with Hugo Ryono.

P-P-P-Pick up an iPad: Zoo unveils latest treat for penguins

A California zoo is believed to be the first in the world to give its penguin residents access to an iPad.

Staff at the Aquarium of the Pacific in Long Beach let two of its Magellanic penguins, Jeremy and Newsom, play on an iPad game originally designed for cats.

The team were astonished when the birds instantly took to the game, chasing an on screen mouse and managing to score highly on the game by tapping their beaks on the screen.

The zoo is trialling the iPad game with its Magellanic penguins, some of which were rescued from Brazil where they were stranded outside their native habitat.

Zoo volunteer Hugo Ryono had the idea after a discussion with keepers about the iPad app 'Game for Cats' and wondered if it could be used as an enrichment aid for the penguins.

'Just like cats, penguins are very curious and the idea of these birds following a virtual mouse on a screen was just too appealing to me not to try out.

'Dusting off my old iPad 1 and loading 'Game for Cats' app on it, we set up a penguin video arcade in the exhibit last week.'

'Sure enough, when Jeremy and Newsom noticed the iPad in the exhibit they both waddled on over. Jeremy was the first to try it out, but Newsom was the one that really got into it.

'Stalking the virtual mouse intently, he tried to pick it up repeatedly with his beak.

'Newsom especially seemed to like the squeak that the mouse made when he put his beak on the virtual critter.

'The mouse was self reinforcing for this penguin.

'Newsom set the penguin high score of 1600 for the game.'

🕒 Extra Time

Watch TV news for a week. What is the funniest 'And finally…' story?

REC

9 Breaking News

↻ Objective

Plan, draft and edit the script for a new lead story.

Breaking news! NASA has made the following announcement:

To: News Reporter

From: News Editor

Dear News Reporter,

Asteroid DA14 is on course to hit the Earth

NASA scientists announced today that their prediction that the 45-metre-wide asteroid would pass 17,200 miles from Earth was incorrect. New measurements show that the asteroid has a 75% chance of entering the Earth's atmosphere within the next 24 hours. Governments around the world have been warned to make preparations for the protection of their citizens against the asteroid strike. NASA have warned that if asteroid DA14 does collide with the Earth it will explode with the force of over 100 atomic bombs. If this explosion takes place over a heavily populated area, the death toll could be in the tens of millions.

Activities

1 You need to write a new lead story for tonight's News Report bulletin. Follow the steps below to start gathering the information you will need.

1 ▶ ## Re-read the announcement from NASA

Make a note of any important points which you think should be included in the news report. Think about who watches News Report, what they will need to know and how you could explain complex information. Could you include interviews with experts, visual tools or presentational techniques? Think how you can help the average viewer understand what might happen.

2 ▶ ## Work in a group

Work in a group to compare the ideas you have gathered in a research conference. Select the best ideas or key pieces of information which you will use to write the lead story script.

Write a first draft of your lead story script. You should:

- Think carefully how to introduce the story. How could you use language to suggest the danger posed by the asteroid and hook your audience from the very start of the report?

- Think about the structure of your news report. Remember to organize your script into paragraphs and note down what will be shown on screen next to each one.

- Use sentence structures and vocabulary to convey information clearly and concisely. Think about how you could include different voices in the report (e.g. the news reporter, expert interviewees, etc.) to help tell the story.

☑ Progress Check

1 Read out first draft to another group, asking them to pick three things that they feel you have done well and things that could be improved.

2 Amend draft in the light of their comments. Proofread check that what you have written is clear and accurate, with correct punctuation and spelling.

3 If possible ICT to present your script. Remember this is to be read aloud in a live news bulletin, so choose style and size that is easy to read.

10 Assessment: Presenting the News

Communicate ideas clearly and speak fluently with appropriate pace, volume and eye contact.

Using the work you have developed throughout this unit, you are going to present a news story on tonight's News Report bulletin. This could be the news story about the asteroid strike from page 128 or any of the other news stories you have worked on in this unit.

The News Report producer wants you to:

- communicate information and ideas clearly
- speak clearly and fluently
- keep the audience's interest.

In particular, they will want to see you:

- selecting an appropriate tone, pace and intonation
- maintaining eye contact with the audience when presenting
- using visual aids and images to support the news report.

ignite INTERVIEW

'Before you address the camera, be in a good mood. Think about a story you really want to tell and the person to whom you want to communicate it is your best friend or a member of your family.'

Will Gompertz

Before you present...

Rehearse: Use the knowled and skills you have learned thr hout this unit. Depending on the ne story you choose, you could work in ually or in a group to rehearse and sent your report. Check your script a hink about the techniques you will us keep the audience's interest.

As you present...

Focus: Take your time: don your nerves make you rush you very of the script. If you make a me, don't worry – just correct yours carry on. Think about your tone of and how you can use intonation to asize key information.

When you have finishe

Reflect: If you have used vi meras to record your news report the report back to evaluate yo rmance. Identify things you have d ll and aspects you would like to i .

GOOD MORNING
NEWS REPORTERS

NR

TODAY'S NEWS...
ASTEROID ATTACK

ON AIR

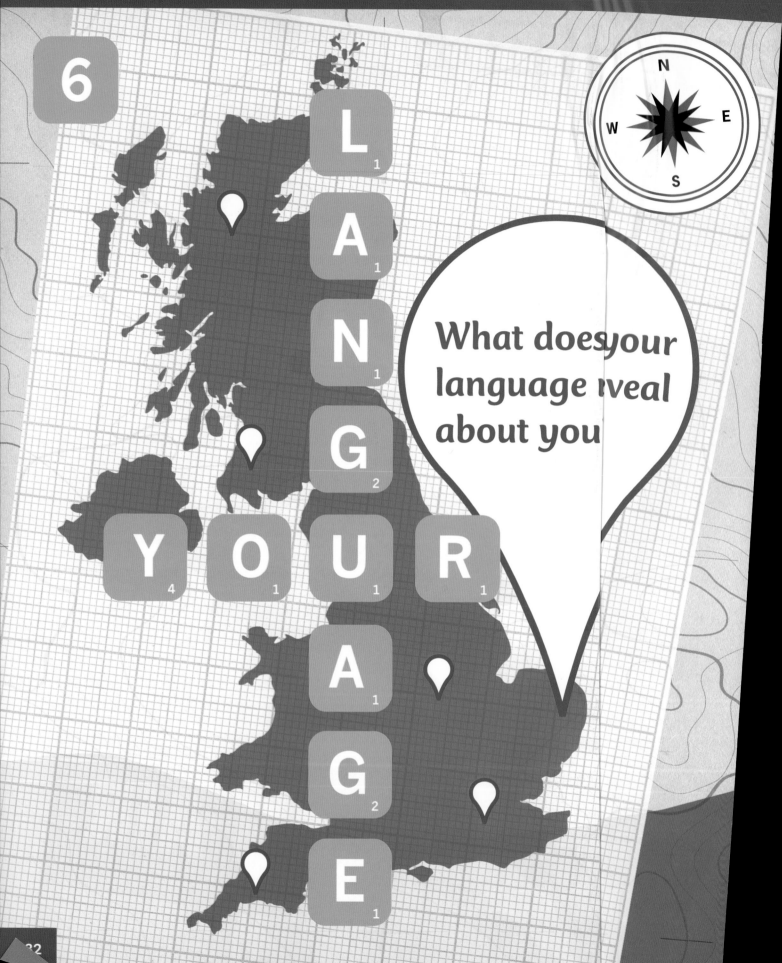

Introduction

Every day, millions of people from all walks of life speak to each other in English, but the language that they use can be very different.

How you use language reflects who you are. It can show where you are from, how old you are and your interests and beliefs. Rightly or wrongly, we often judge people by the way that they speak.

In this unit, you will explore why spoken language varies so much. You will discover that some people have very strong views about 'right' and 'wrong' language and you will have an opportunity to express your own views.

The East

The West

ignite INTERVIEW
Maeve Diamond, Accent and dialect coach

An accent is how we pronounce our words, whereas a dialect is the words that we choose. I think we are fascinated by accents because we are fascinated by difference. It is fascinating to hear and study how other people speak and how even though they speak differently, most of the time we understand exactly what they mean. Pronunciation can change within an accent, but it is not just vowels and consonants in pronunciation that change. As well as our **rhythm**, we also have **pitch** and **intonation** changes. What I love about the range of accents in the UK and throughout the world is the variety and the detail of the changes.

✎ Activities

1 How many different words can you think of that mean 'hello' and 'goodbye'? What situations would you use these different words in?

2 Why do we use different language with different people? Identify at least four different situations, and decide why you use different language in each of these situations.

📖 Glossary

rhythm   a regularly repeated beat

pitch   how high or low your voice is

intonation   the rise and fall of a person's voice when they speak

1 It's a What?

↻ Objective

Understand differences between dialect, slang and Standard English.

Spoken language varies from place to place. People from different places sometimes use different words to describe the same thing. For example, a narrow public footpath between houses is called a 'ginnel' in Manchester and a 'snickleway' in York.

These words are examples of **dialect**. Dialect words are usually spoken, are usually informal and tend to be used in a specific geographical area. Regional dialects can also include adding in words in an unusual grammatical way. For example, in Tyneside (in north-east England) the word 'man' is often added at the end of sentences, even when the conversation is not directed at a man!

Language can also vary depending upon social groups and the situation in which people are speaking. One example of this is **slang**. Slang is often, though not always, used by a particular group of people, for example teenagers. Slang is very informal and is not usually linked to a specific geographical area (unlike dialect). An example of slang could be 'cool', which is often used to mean 'great'.

However there is a variety of English language that is the same wherever it is used, and that is known as **Standard English**. Standard English tends to be more formal and is regarded as the 'correct' form of words. So, in the example above, 'footpath' is Standard English.

✎ Activities

1a Look at items A to C below. Decide which of the scattered words link to each item. Add more words if you can.

1b Which word in each group would you be most likely to use?

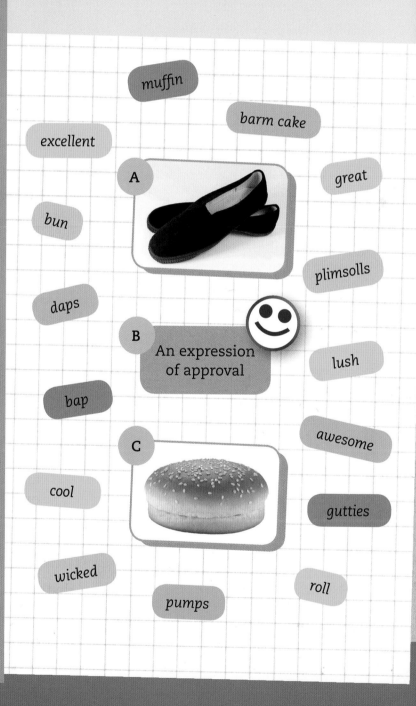

muffin

barm cake

excellent

A

great

bun

plimsolls

daps

B
An expression of approval

lush

bap

awesome

C

cool

gutties

wicked

roll

pumps

2 Look at the expressions on the right. Can you work out what each one means?

In the past, most people spoke with some sort of regional dialect. Nowadays, some people believe dialects are becoming less distinct. There are lots of reasons for this:

- National TV and radio programmes are broadcast all over the country, so regional dialect and slang are replaced by Standard English which everyone knows and recognizes.

- People move around more, share their dialect and adapt it to new places, so the dialect becomes less distinct.

- Older people tend to use dialect more than younger people so, as the older generation dies, dialect is used less and less.

'a right bobby dazzler'

'Keep your neb out!'

3 List the pros and cons of dialect and slang words. When might they be appropriate? When might they cause problems?

4 What situations can you think of where Standard English might be appropriate? Why?

📖 Glossary

dialect informal words used in a specific geographical area

slang informal words typically used by specific groups but not in a specific geographical area

Standard English the variety of English that is regarded as 'correct' and is used in more formal situations. It is not specific to any geographical area and can be spoken or written.

2 It's My Accent

↻ Objective

Explore attitudes to different accents.

As well as using different words and expressions, people often *pronounce* language differently. The same word may have the same spelling but may *sound* different in various parts of the country. These variations are called **accents** and everyone has one. The Queen speaks in **Received Pronunciation (RP)**, whereas the TV presenters Ant and Dec have Newcastle or Geordie accents.

A **linguist** called Howard Giles carried out some research on accents. He found that people tend to trust people with certain accents more than others. He discovered that most people warm towards people who have rural accents rather than city accents.

✎ Activities

1a Look at the grid below and decide how you feel about different accents. For each category, choose 1 if you strongly disagree and 5 if you strongly agree.

1b Compare your results with a partner. Talk about why you agree and why you differ.

↔ Stretch

Discuss how people's preferences for certain accents might affect the voices we hear on TV or radio. How might their roles differ, for example presenting the news or the weather?

Accent	Friendly (1-5)	Intelligent (1-5)	Trustworthy (1-5)
RP			
Brummie (Birmingham)			
Estuary (London and Essex)			
Geordie (Newcastle)			
Scouse (Liverpool)			
West Country			

Some linguists create maps to show where different accents and dialects are used. This helps us to understand how people use language today and also helps to track how our language is changing.

2 You are contributing to an accent map of Great Britain. Working in pairs or small groups, choose an area of the country (this could be where you live). Brainstorm and then jot down some of the features of the accent for that area. For instance, 'path' and 'grass' in the north of England have a short 'a' sound like in 'h<u>a</u>t'.

ignite INTERVIEW

'What I love about the range of accents in the UK and throughout the world is the variety. You can go a very short journey and you could find that the inhabitants of that local area can sound markedly different from wherever you have come from initially.'

Maeve Diamond

📖 Glossary

accent   way of pronouncing language

Received Pronunciation (RP)   the 'standard' form of pronunciation, not linked to a particular area; often seen as the prestige (poshest) accent of English

linguist   someone who studies how language is used

☑ Progress Check

Copy out the grid below. Think about each statement and decide how confident you are. Then write an explanation giving examples for each one.

Statement	Yes	Fairly sure	No	Explanation
I know what a dialect is.				A dialect is...
I know what slang is.				Slang is...
I know what an accent is.				An accent is...
I can give examples of dialect words.				1 2 3
I can give examples of slang words.				1 2 3
I can name some different accents.				1 2 3

Extra Time

Ask your family and friends to complete the accent-ratings grid from Activity 1a. Then think of an interesting way to present your findings to the class.

③ Spoken Language in Literature

↻ Objective

Investigate how spoken language is represented in literary texts.

It can be difficult for writers to show dialect and accent in writing. Linguists use the **phonetic alphabet** to show how words are pronounced, but most people can't read phonetics. Some fiction writers use **eye dialect** instead. This shows us how a character sounds when they speak, which helps us to understand where they are from and what kind of person they might be.

Extract from
'Oh, I Wish I'd Looked After Me Teeth'
by Pam Ayres

Oh, I wish I'd looked after me teeth,

And spotted the dangers beneath

All the toffees I chewed,

And the sweet sticky food.

Oh, I wish I'd looked after me teeth.

I wish I'd been that much more willin'

When I had more tooth there than fillin'

To give up gobstoppers,

From respect to me choppers,

And to buy something else with me shillin'.

✏ Activities

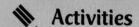

1a Look at the extract from the poem by Pam Ayres.

Pick out the examples of eye dialect.

1b Discuss why you think the speaker in the poem chose to use eye dialect. Talk about:

- what the poet wanted the reader to understand about the speaker in the poem

- what effect the use of eye dialect has on the reader.

1c The apostrophe can be used to show possession (belonging) or contraction (when one or more letters are missing). What contraction apostrophes in this poem are commonplace and which are used to show pronunciation? **SPAG**

📖 Glossary

phonetic alphabet   symbols to show how words are pronounced, e.g. 'sheep' is written phonetically as /ʃïp/ and 'ship' as /ʃɪp/

eye dialect   words written to show how they should sound rather than using the correct spelling, e.g. 'dahn' instead of 'down'

Read the text below. It is from a novel called *Wuthering Heights*, by Emily Brontë. Joseph is a servant in a large remote house called Wuthering Heights. Mr Lockwood is staying in another large house nearby and has come to visit Joseph's master. He is not expected at this time.

2a What kind of place do you think the story is set in? What makes you think that?

2b What kind of person do you think the writer wants us to think of when we hear Joseph speak? What makes you think that?

2c How does Mr Lockwood's speech contrast with Joseph's? (Mr Lockwood is the narrator, so uses the word 'I'.)

Extract from *Wuthering Heights* by Emily Brontë

Vinegar-faced Joseph projected his head from a round window of the barn.

'Whet are ye for?' he shouted. 'T' maister's dahn i' t' fowld. Go a rahnd by th' end ut' laith, if yah went tuh spake tull him.'

Sheep pen

Barn

'Is there nobody inside to open the door?' I hallooed, responsively.

'They's nobbut t' missis; and shoo'll nut oppen't an ye mak yer flaysome dins till neeght.'

Frightening noise

Support

Some expressions are tricky to work out if you are not familiar with the dialect. Here are some clues:

'The master'

'What are you doing here?'

'until night time'

'There's no one apart from the lady of the house'

More to explore

When we read a text which includes dialect and eye dialect, it helps us to feel that we are seeing and hearing the events 'live'. However, it can also cause difficulties if the reader cannot follow the text easily.

Writers sometimes use eye dialect in non-fiction in order to create a strong impression of the place and people. Read the extract on the opposite page. It is from an autobiography called *Cider With Rosie*.

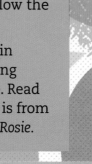 Activities continued

3a Pick out any dialect, slang and eye dialect words in the extract opposite.

3b Which of the examples show accent and which show dialect?

3c Rewrite the dialect and eye dialect in Standard English. For example: 'you ain't' is an example of a dialect term which would be written 'aren't' or 'are not' in Standard English.

Remember, Standard English is the form of English language that is generally used for formal purposes in speech and writing. It is not the English of any particular region and it can be spoken with any accent.

4 Thinking about the example texts in this lesson (on pages 138, 139 and 141), do you think they would be more effective written in Standard English? Explain your views to a partner, or write them down, supporting your ideas with evidence from the texts.

Support

Choose one of the prose texts (either *Wuthering Heights* or *Cider With Rosie*) and explain whether or not you found it easy to read. Identify the words you found easy to understand and which ones you found hard. Explain why.

The author of this extract, Laurie Lee, writes about his childhood in Gloucestershire just after the First World War. In this extract, he is describing life at primary school. Some of the narrative is written in Standard English from the point of view of the adult Laurie, but some of the direct speech is written in eye dialect, so we can 'hear' the voices of the children from the past.

Extract from *Cider With Rosie*

by Laurie Lee

Sometimes there was a beating, which nobody minded – except an occasional red-faced mother. Sometimes a man came and took out our teeth. ('My mum says you ain't to take out any double'uns…' '… Fourteen, fifteen, sixteen, seventeen…' 'Is they all double-uns?' 'Shut up, you little horror.') Sometimes the Squire would pay us a visit, hand out prizes, and make a misty-eyed speech. Sometimes an Inspector arrived on a bicycle and counted our heads and departed. Meanwhile Miss Wardley moved jingling amongst us, instructing, appealing, despairing:

'You're a grub, Walter Kerry. You have the wits of a hen. You're a great hulking lout of an oaf. You can just stay behind and do it over again. You can all stay behind, the lot of you.'

When lessons grew too tiresome, or too insoluble, we had our traditional ways of avoiding them.

'Please, miss, I got to stay 'ome tomorrow, to 'elp with the washing – the pigs – me dad's sick.'

'I dunno, miss; you never learned us that.'

'I 'ad me book stole, miss. Carry Burdock pinched it.'

'Please, miss, I got a gurt 'eadache.'

Sometimes these worked, sometimes they didn't. But once, when some tests hung over our heads, a group of us boys evaded them entirely by stinging our hands with horseflies. The task took all day, but the results were spectacular – our hands swelled like elephants' trunks.

''Twas a swarm, please, miss. They set on us. We run, but they stung us awful.' I remember how we groaned, and that we couldn't hold our pens but I don't remember the pain.

🕒 Extra Time

Write a short text in which you use eye dialect in direct speech to show a sense of character and place.

4 Join Our Club

↻ Objective

Explore the language of specific social groups.

Do you have a hobby? Do you play for a sports team? Are you into a particular kind of music? If your answer to any of these questions is 'yes', then you probably use a **sociolect**, which is the particular language of a social group. People who don't have the same interests won't use the same sociolect.

✎ Activities

1 Look at the words below. They each belong to a sociolect linked to a specific activity. Match each word to the correct category: ballet, skateboarding or football.

2 Choose a hobby or interest that you have (or would like to have) and list the specialist words or phrases that you use linked to that hobby or interest. Write a definition for each, making the meaning clear to someone who has a different sociolect.

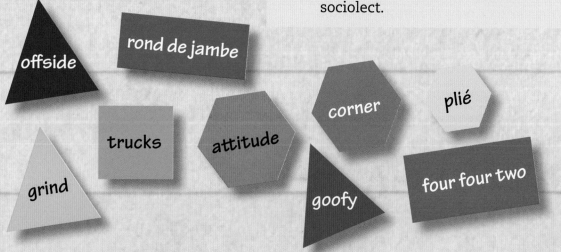

offside

rond de jambe

trucks

attitude

corner

plié

grind

goofy

four four two

The author of this extract is a climber. He and his climbing partner are ice-climbing in the French Alps.

Extract from *The Beckoning Silence* by Joe Simpson

I looked down at where I had placed my last ice screw in a boss of water ice **protruding** from a fractured and melting ice wall 35 feet below me. If I fell now I would drop 80 feet and I knew the ice screw would not hold me. The ice boss would shatter and it would be instantly ripped out. It had quickly become apparent that the route was in poor condition. Lower down I had found myself moving from solid ice onto a strange skim of water ice overlaying soft, sugary snow. It was just strong enough to hold my axe picks and crampon points but it would never hold an ice screw. Hoping for an improvement I had climbed higher and moved diagonally towards the right side of the wall. Then the ice began to resemble something more commonly found furring up the icebox in my fridge. I moved tentatively over rotten honeycombed water ice and onto frightening near-vertical slabs of rime ice – a feathery concoction of hoarfrost and loosely bonded powder snow.

3 Pick out any words or phrases that are part of a sociolect shared by people with similar interests. Can you work out what each of the terms might mean, using the context (surrounding text) to help you?

Social groups can be linked by more than just a hobby or interest. They can be linked by gender, age, education, social background or religious beliefs. Each group has its own sociolect, with members sharing many of the same words, phrases and expressions.

4a Discuss the pros and cons of people using sociolect terms. (Think about what feelings you might trigger if you use words that some people don't understand, but others do.)

4b You are creating a glossary for newcomers to a club. Write two paragraphs explaining the benefits and drawbacks of a sociolect. Try to be specific, giving examples of sociolect words and expressions.

📖 Glossary

sociolect a variety of language used by a particular social group

protruding sticking out

ROCK ROCKS

5 It's Just Idiolect!

↺ Objective

Explain the features that make up your own idiolect.

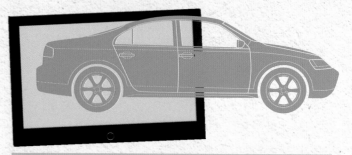

You have learned that everyone's language is influenced by their accent, dialect and sociolect. All these things build up a very individual pattern of language that is different for each person. It is called their **idiolect**. A person's idiolect is as unique as a fingerprint and can tell us a great deal about them.

Some people consciously choose words and phrases for their idiolect to try to make a certain impression on other people. They might use phrases from their favourite TV show or celebrity catchphrases to associate themselves with that person and their way of life.

✎ Activities

1 Consider each of the characters listed below. Think about the factors that will make up their idiolect.

- A teacher from Gloucestershire. He likes golf and rugby, and watches Top Gear every week.

- A teenager from London. She likes pop music and watches lots of soaps on TV.

- A granny from Scotland. She likes knitting and surfing the net.

Look at the spider diagram drawn for the teacher. It shows some likely features of his idiolect. Draw similar spider diagrams for the teenager and the granny, suggesting words, where possible, and phrases that they may use.

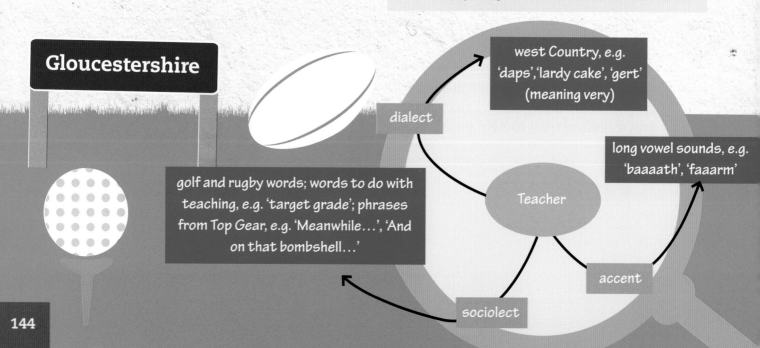

Gloucestershire

dialect — west Country, e.g. 'daps', 'lardy cake', 'gert' (meaning very)

accent — long vowel sounds, e.g. 'baaaath', 'faaarm'

sociolect — golf and rugby words; words to do with teaching, e.g. 'target grade'; phrases from Top Gear, e.g. 'Meanwhile...', 'And on that bombshell...'

Teacher

2a Now think about yourself. What are the main influences on your idiolect? Make a list of them.

2b For each factor that influences your idiolect, write down one or two examples of language that you use. Then, for each example, write a brief explanation of when you would use it and why. Use a grid like the one below to show your information.

Influences on idiolect	Examples	Explanation
Dialect	'bairn', 'wee', 'loch'	I live in Scotland and I use these words to mean 'baby', 'small' and 'lake'.
Hobbies: skateboarding, football, fishing		

3a Share your language profile that you wrote in Activity 2b with a partner. Ask them to add anything that they may have noticed about your idiolect, for example catchphrases that you often use.

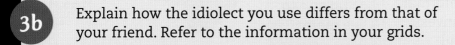

Know what I mean?

Awesome!

Go for it...

3b Explain how the idiolect you use differs from that of your friend. Refer to the information in your grids.

☑ Progress Check

Write a **tweet** (using a maximum of 140 characters) starting: 'My idiolect is unique because…'.

Share your tweet with a partner. Decide which gives the clearest, most accurate summary of idiolect and why. Rate your own tweet on a scale of 1 to 3 (3 being the highest score).

📖 Glossary

idiolect   the language pattern of an individual person

tweet   a short message with a maximum of 140 characters used in the social networking site Twitter

6 Proper Posh

↻ Objective

Discover the differences between formal and informal language.

During the course of just one day, you will use and hear lots of different types of language. It will vary from **formal** to **informal**, depending on who you are with, where you are and what you are doing.

✎ Activities

1 In some situations we need to use formal language, while in others it is acceptable to use informal language. What level of formality do you think would be most appropriate in the situations on the right? Explain your answers.

📖 Glossary

formal language follows grammatical rules and uses Standard English

informal language tends to use non-standard English, such as slang words and non-standard grammar, e.g. informal speech might include double negatives: *We didn't see nothing*, or the verb and subject may not agree: *We was lucky to get away with it.*

Texting a friend

Talking in a job interview

Writing a report

Talking to a judge in court

Writing a newspaper article

Talking to a teacher

Talking to a mate

Phoning a brother or sister

Talking to a police officer

2 Informal spoken language includes features that we rarely see in formal spoken language or in formal writing. Some of these features are listed in the Glossary box on page 146. Link each feature below to the correct example in the speech bubbles on the right. (Some examples may contain more than one feature.)

tag questions questions added to the end of a sentence to turn it from a statement into a question

contractions words or phrases that are shortened by missing out letters and replacing them with an apostrophe

slang casual non-standard words, often used by a social group

fillers words which are used to fill pauses

> Don't give any money.

> I am skint.

> It's hot, isn't it?

> I was freezing, you know.

3 Read the **transcript** below.

Last year was like wicked. I went to the Olympics in London and it was well cool. The best bit was getting to see Usain Bolt, you know what I mean? It's like, I dunno, a once in a lifetime thing. Never gonna get the chance to do that again, am I? And it was the Queen's thing as well, right. We got an extra day off school for that. Awesome.

Pick out examples of informal language and explain what they are and how they differ from Standard English.

📖 Glossary

transcript a written copy of something spoken

More to explore

People in authority tend to use formal language when addressing meetings, the public or the media. Their speeches are often written down first and rewritten many times before they are actually spoken. Often, the speaker rehearses them.

This is an extract from the Queen's Christmas message in 2012. This was a year in which she celebrated her Diamond Jubilee and the London Olympics took place.

H.M. The Queen

Buckingham Palace, London

This past year has been one of great celebration for many. The enthusiasm which greeted the Diamond Jubilee was, of course, especially memorable for me and my family. It was humbling that so many chose to mark the anniversary of a duty which passed to me 60 years ago. People of all ages took the trouble to take part in various ways and in many nations. But perhaps most striking of all was to witness the strength of fellowship and friendship among those who had gathered together on these occasions.

Activities continued

4 Look closely at the Queen's speech. On a scale of 1 to 5 (with 1 being very informal and 5 being very formal), how would you rate the Queen's speech?

5 How do the following differ between the Queen's speech and the transcript (on page 147):

- the vocabulary (choice of words)
- the type of English used (Standard or non-standard)
- the variety of sentence structures, for example the use of **subordinate clauses**?

SPAG

Spoken, everyday language is usually more informal than written language. However, sometimes we have to 'translate' from one to the other. For example, imagine a teacher is off sick and cannot finish writing all the school reports for her class. The Head Teacher listens to the teacher briefly on the phone to get an idea of what to write in the teacher's absence. Read the transcript below.

Mark can never shut up. He's always talking and no one else can concentrate when he is in class. Luckily, he's a big skiver, so he's not here very often.

His spelling is dire and his handwriting looks like a spider fell in some ink, do you know what I mean? He is always full of excuses for why he hasn't done his homework.

6 Re-write this transcript into a formal written report.

📚 Support

Remember, formal language should not include slang or informal expressions. It should be written in Standard English.

📖 Glossary

main clause   a clause that can stand alone and make sense without any other clauses

subordinate clause   a clause that supports the **main clause** in giving further explanation or detail, but cannot stand alone. It may start with words such as 'which', 'who', 'that' or 'when'.

For example:

The winner of the lottery was Iona Rolls, who lived in the same street as me.

Main Clause

Subordinate Clause

☑ Progress Check

Think about the different levels of formality in the language that you use in a day. Write a short paragraph to explain how and why the levels of formality in your spoken language change throughout the day.

🕐 Extra Time

Record a brief conversation with friends. Transcribe the conversation, highlighting examples of informal language.

HIGHLIGHTS

7 An Idiot's Guide to Spoken Language

↻ Objective

Analyse the key features of an information text.

Think about how much you have learned about spoken language in this unit. It's time to put your knowledge to the test and help other people to learn as much as you have.

Good information texts present complex topics in a simple way. Some are more formal than others, but they all have the same aim: to teach their reader something.

A popular title for some information texts is 'An Idiot's Guide to…', which is designed for people who have little or no knowledge about a subject. Although these information texts, for example health leaflets in doctors' surgeries, can be written in quite a humorous way, they still need to present the information clearly and effectively.

✎ Activities

1 Discuss information texts and list some key features that they use. Think about:

- how information can be divided up
- the style of language they are written in (formal or informal)
- different ways of conveying information, for example visuals as well as text.

2 Your task is to plan and create 'An Idiot's Guide to Spoken Language' for sharing with students in other classes to help improve their understanding. You will need to make notes about:

- key points that you want your reader to learn
- how you will divide your material under headings
- technical words that you will need to explain in a glossary
- examples or case studies that you will use
- illustrations you might include.

🗂 Support

Your notes could take the form of a spider diagram, like the one started below. This will help you structure your notes.

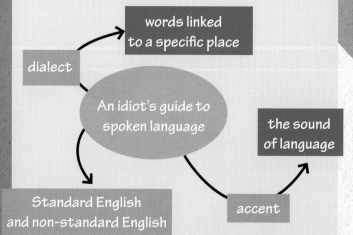

- dialect
- words linked to a specific place
- An idiot's guide to spoken language
- the sound of language
- accent
- Standard English and non-standard English

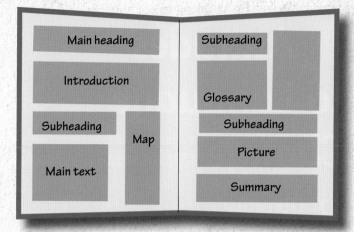

3 Next, plan the layout of your guide, deciding where to put the different features, keeping in mind the purpose and audience for your guide. It might help to annotate a sketch of your layout, like the one on the right.

4 When you have decided on your content and layout, write your version of 'An Idiot's Guide to Spoken Language'.

5 Real writers have to make sure their work is perfect before it is published, so take time to finalize your text. Once you have finished, proofread your work with care, using a dictionary if necessary and checking the grammar is accurate. You might want to use a computer to present your final work.

↔ Stretch

Write a commentary that explains the decisions you made in creating your information text. Include:

- why you chose the information that you included
- how you chose to present your information
- why you chose the **tone** that you did and what effect it has
- how you wrote with a specific purpose and audience in mind.

☑ Progress Check

Swap your work with a partner. Check each other's information text to see whether you have achieved the success criteria listed below. For each criterion, note whether it is:

- totally achieved
- partly achieved
- not achieved.

Success criteria

- The guide includes the key features of an information text, e.g. introduction, glossary, headings.
- The guide is written in an appropriate style.
- The guide includes the technical terms of language, e.g. dialect, sociolect, accent, idiolect.
- The guide is clear and easy to follow.
- The guide suits its purpose: to inform.

📖 Glossary

tone   the way words are spoken, e.g. a serious tone, a light-hearted tone, etc.

151

8 Attitudes to Language Change

↻ Objective

Identify different views about language change.

Language is something that we all use, and many people have strong opinions about it. Some people believe that certain words, expressions and pronunciations are 'right' and others are 'wrong'.

Opinions about language tend to fit into one of two groups: people who think that language has strict rules which should never change or be broken; and people who think that language changes all the time and that diversity is a good thing.

✎ Activities

1 Look at the statements on this page and decide which of the two types of people might have said them (people who think that language has strict rules or people who think that language changes all the time).

2 Decide whether you agree or disagree with each statement. Explain why.

Language grows and changes – it always has done and it always will.

Kids these days can't spell – it's all because of too much texting.

It's boring if everyone talks in exactly the same way.

Dialect words should be banned in schools. Children should be learning Standard English only.

People take more notice of people who speak 'properly'.

Young people often introduce new words into the language – it keeps it lively!

Young people are so disrespectful – I can't tell what they are saying half the time.

Written and spoken language is affected by historical events. Look at the fact flashes below.

In 1476, William Caxton brought the first printing press to England. This helped to standardize the English language. Before printing, books had previously been written by hand.

William Shakespeare wrote in the late 16th and early 17th centuries. He made up lots of new words and phrases which we still use today, such as 'more fool you'.

New inventions require different forms of language. Text messages use abbreviated language for speed, e.g. 'LOL'.

In 1755, Samuel Johnson wrote the first major dictionary. It clarified spellings, gave definitions and included more than just 'tricky' words, unlike previous dictionaries.

In the 18th century, people began to write grammar books to set down the 'rules' for using English correctly.

New inventions bring new vocabulary, e.g. hoover, biro, bicycle, the worldwide web, googling.

3 Discuss each of the fact flashes above. What do you think they tell us about how the language we use today has been influenced? (Think about written and spoken language.)

4 Some people think that set rules of language should always be followed, for example, spelling, punctuation and grammatical correctness. What are the advantages of having such rules? When do you think they can be broken?

5 Write a short presentation about language change. It should focus on why and how language changes, as well as the value of keeping some aspects of language 'fixed' through rules. Use statements like those started below. Use slides or prompts that contain one statement that you can explain further.

New inventions affect language because…
Using Standard English is helpful when…

To help inform your presentation try to do some research.

9 Stand Up for Language!

↻ Objective

Form a personal view about language varieties.

People have very different ideas about what is 'right' and 'wrong' with language today. Some people believe that everyone should try to speak and write in Standard English, whereas others believe that variety in language should be encouraged and celebrated. You need to decide what your personal views are and be prepared to present them.

✎ Activities

1 Read what different people have said about language in the speech bubbles on the right and then rank the statements according to how true you think they are.

2 When you have ranked your statements, share your work with a partner. Discuss any differences of opinion that you have.

ignite INTERVIEW

'I think we are so fascinated by accents because we are fascinated by difference. If we were all the same, life would be really boring.'

Maeve Diamond

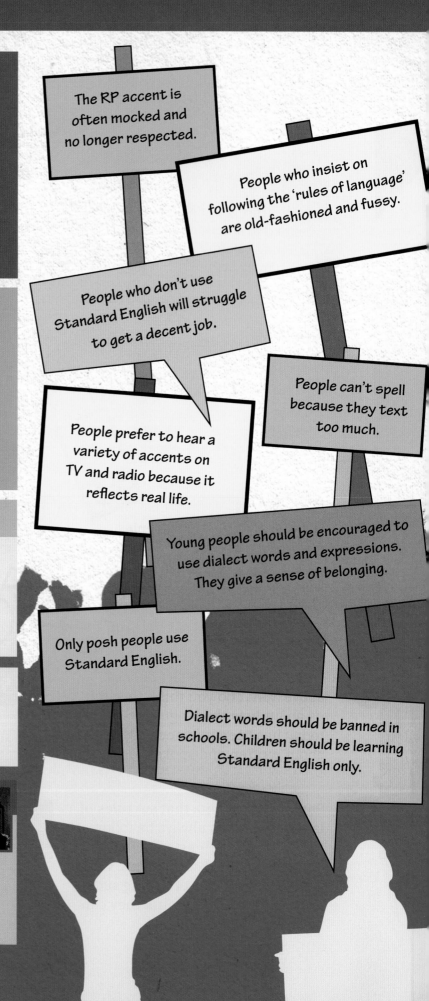

The RP accent is often mocked and no longer respected.

People who insist on following the 'rules of language' are old-fashioned and fussy.

People who don't use Standard English will struggle to get a decent job.

People can't spell because they text too much.

People prefer to hear a variety of accents on TV and radio because it reflects real life.

Young people should be encouraged to use dialect words and expressions. They give a sense of belonging.

Only posh people use Standard English.

Dialect words should be banned in schools. Children should be learning Standard English only.

The extract below appeared in a news article in the *Evening Gazette* in Middlesbrough.

MIDDLESBROUGH SCHOOL URGES PARENTS TO CORRECT PUPILS' TEES DIALECT

Parents have been asked to ensure their children use the Queen's English [Standard English], rather than a more "Teeside" version.

A letter sent home to parents whose children attend Sacred Heart Primary School in Middlesbrough gives advice about pronunciation and grammar.

It details several phrases which are often used in class but need correcting – and many will be familiar to Teessiders!

Some aim for grammatical accuracy – the correct use of "your" and "you're" for example.

But others have a distinct Teesside twang to them – take the phrase "I will wear my shirt for work" rather than using "shert" and "werk".

"I done that" and "I seen that" may be used in the playground, but they're a "no no" in the exercise book. And school DOESN'T finish at "free fifteen" – it finishes at three fifteen!

If yous lot reading this think "yous" is a correct term, think again. And you'd betta believe it – it's "butter" and "letter" not "butta" and "letta"!

3 Why do you think the Head Teacher believes children should be encouraged to speak Standard English? Which explanation below do you think is most likely? (There may be more than one.)

- She isn't from Teeside, so probably can't understand what her pupils are saying.

- She is worried that regional dialects and accents are dying out and fewer people can understand them.

- She thinks people will make unfair judgements about the pupils if they use a lot of dialect words and expressions, and pronounce things with a strong regional accent.

4 Imagine that you are a parent with children at this school. Would you do what the Head Teacher suggests, or would you disagree? Discuss either in pairs or as a class and then explain your point of view in a brief letter to the school.

Your letter might start:

Dear Head Teacher,

Thank you for your letter about encouraging children to use Standard English. I agree/disagree with your view because…

10 Assessment: Plan, Draft and Edit a Presentation about Language

You have been asked to contribute to a TV programme about spoken language. It is a panel show in which different people are asked to give their views about whether students should be made to speak and write in Standard English while at school.

Here is an email from the producer of the show:

What do you think?

RE: Real Language TV Show ★

Hi!

Thanks for agreeing to take part in *It's My Language* at AJS Productions. After the recent reports about schools asking parents to encourage the use of Standard English at home as well as at school, we are aware that many people have very strong views on this subject. We'd really like to hear what you think, particularly from your viewpoint as a student.

You will have a maximum of five minutes to present your views and then there will be a general discussion among all our panellists, so be prepared to answer questions and support your ideas with examples. Please note that you will be our first speaker. Some of our audience are quite young and don't have much knowledge about language, so you will need to explain any special terms that you use, such as Standard English, dialect, accent, slang, etc.

We are looking forward to hearing your views!

Your task is to plan, draft and edit a presentation for this TV programme, using the knowledge and skills that you have gained from this unit.

The producer will want you to:

- introduce the topic of language, explaining how some people feel that some language is 'correct' and some 'incorrect'

- give a clear explanation about the difference between Standard English and non-standard English

- give examples of non-standard English, such as dialect, accent, slang, tag questions, fillers, etc.

- give your views about the use of Standard English – whether it should be encouraged at school, in written or spoken language, or whether diversity in language should be celebrated and encouraged.

Remember, for a presentation you should:

- group your ideas into paragraphs that flow on from each other

- explain any terms that may be unfamiliar to viewers

- use clear, accessible language, giving examples where possible.

Before you write…

Planning: Use the knowledge and skills you have learned throughout this unit. Re-read the producer's email, thinking about your audience and your task.

Think about the structure of your presentation. It should have a clear introduction, then paragraphs about different ideas and a conclusion. You may wish to use a few visuals to illustrate what you are saying.

As you write…

Reviewing and editing: Check that you are following your plan, keeping your aims in mind, reading and re-reading what you have written to make sure it is clear and makes sense.

Check that you are explaining any terms that may be unfamiliar to your audience, and giving examples to show what you mean.

When you have finished writing…

Proofreading: Check that what you have written is clear and accurate, with correct punctuation and spelling. You may wish to highlight key words that you want to emphasize.

If possible, use a computer to present your final work, so that your script is as clear and easy to follow as possible.

Rehearse your speech, to make sure your sentences flow easily and your explanations sound clear.

KS3 National Curriculum and *Ignite English* mapping: **Reading**

National Curriculum: subject content	Unit 1: In Search of Adventure	Unit 2: The Identity Kit	Unit 3: Out of this World	Unit 4: Travellers' Tales	Unit 5: Making the News	Unit 6: Your Language
Develop an appreciation and love of reading and read increasingly challenging material independently — Reading a wide range of fiction and non-fiction, including in particular whole books, short stories, poems and plays with a wide coverage of genres, historical periods, forms and authors. The range will include high-quality works from:	L1, L2, L4, L5, L6, L7, L8, L9	L1, L3, L5, L6, L7, L8, L9, L10	L2, L3, L4, L5, L6, L7, L8	L1, L2, L3, L4, L5, L6, L7	L1, L4, L7, L8	L3, L4, L9
• English literature, both pre-1914 and contemporary, including prose, poetry and drama	L2, L5	L1, L3, L5, L6, L7, L8, L9, L10	L2, L3, L6, L7	L1, L7		L2 (TC), L3
• Shakespeare (two plays)			L9			
• seminal world literature		L4, L7				
Choosing and reading books independently for challenge, interest and enjoyment		L4 (TC)				
Re-reading books encountered earlier to increase familiarity with them and provide a basis for making comparisons		L2				
Understand increasingly challenging texts — Learning new vocabulary, relating it explicitly to known vocabulary and understanding it with the help of context and dictionaries	L4, L5	L1, L3 (TC), L7 (TC), L8	L2, L3, L4, L6 (TC)	L1, L7	L3, L5 (TC)	L3, L4
Making inferences and referring to evidence in the text	L2, L3, L4, L5, L6, L7, L9	L4, L5, L8	L2, L5, L7, L8, L9	L2, L5	L1	L3
Knowing the purpose, audience for and context of the writing and drawing on this knowledge to support comprehension	L3, L4, L6, L7, L8	L5, L9, L10	L3	L2, L4, L7	L3, L5, L7	
Checking their understanding to make sure that what they have read makes sense	L2, L3, L4	L4, L10	L4, L7, L9	L5	L9	L3
Read critically — Knowing how language, including figurative language, vocabulary choice, grammar, text structure and organizational features, presents meaning	L1, L2, L5, L6, L7, L8, L9	L1, L2, L4, L5, L6, L7, L8	L1, L2, L3, L6, L7, L9	L1, L2, L3, L4, L6, L7	L3, L5	L3, L4
Recognizing a range of poetic conventions and understanding how these have been used	L4	L1, L2, L3, L5, L6, L8, L9, L10				
Studying setting, plot and characterization, and the effects of these	L1, L2, L3, L5, L7	L2, L4, L10	L2, L4 (TC), L6, L7, L9	L1, L2 (TC)	L3	
Understanding how the work of dramatists is communicated effectively through performance and how alternative staging allows for different interpretations of a play			L9, L3 (TC)			
Making critical comparisons across texts	L5					
Studying a range of authors, including at least two authors in depth each year	L2, L3, L4, L5, L9	L1, L2, L3, L4, L5, L6, L7, L8, L9, L10	L2, L3, L5, L6, L7, L9	L1, L2, L5, L6, L7		L3, L4

Key: L = Lesson (Student Book); TC = Teacher Companion

KS3 National Curriculum and *Ignite English* mapping: **Writing**

National Curriculum: subject content		Unit 1: In Search of Adventure	Unit 2: The Identity Kit	Unit 3: Out of this World	Unit 4: Travellers' Tales	Unit 5: Making the News	Unit 6: Your Language
Write accurately, fluently, effectively and at length for pleasure and information	Writing for a wide range of purposes and audiences, including:						
	• well-structured formal expository and narrative essays	L6			L6		L6 (TC)
	• stories, scripts, poetry and other imaginative writing	L3, L5, L7 (TC)	L3, L4, L6, L8 (TC)	L2, L3, L6, L7, L9, L10	L5 (TC), L7	L5	
	• notes and polished scripts for talks and presentations			L5	L1, L4, L8	L6, L8, L9	L5 (TC), L8, L10
	• a range of other narrative and non-narrative texts, including arguments, and personal and formal letters	L2 (TC), L7, L7 (TC), L8 (TC), L9	L1, L2 (TC), L7, L10	L4, L8	L2, L3	L2, L3	L3, L9
	Summarizing and organizing material, and supporting ideas and arguments with any necessary factual detail	L1, L2 (TC), L8	L9		L2, L6	L2 (TC), L5, L6, L8, L9	L7, L9, L10
	Applying their growing knowledge of vocabulary, grammar and text structure to their writing, and selecting the appropriate form	L1, L5, L6	L4, L8 (TC)	L2, L3, L6, L7, L10	L3, L6, L7, L8	L3, L5, L8, L9	L3 (TC), L7, L10
	Drawing on knowledge of literary and rhetorical devices from their reading and listening to enhance the impact of their writing	L5, L6	L2, L3, L4, L6, L7	L2, L6, L7, L10	L6, L7, L8		
Plan, draft, edit and proofread	Considering how their writing reflects the audiences and purposes for which it was intended	L6 (TC)	L4	L7, L8, L10		L5, L9	L7, L10
	Amending the vocabulary, grammar and structure of their writing to improve its coherence and overall effectiveness	L6 (TC)	L4	L7, L10	L1 (TC)	L5, L9	L7, L10
	Paying attention to accurate grammar, punctuation and spelling; applying the spelling patterns and rules set out in English Appendix 1 to the Key Stage 1 and 2 programmes of study for English	L9 (TC)	L10 (TC)	L10	L8, L8 (TC)		L10

Key: L = Lesson (Student Book); TC = Teacher Companion

KS3 National Curriculum and *Ignite English* mapping: **Grammar and vocabulary**

National Curriculum: subject content	Unit 1: In Search of Adventure	Unit 2: The Identity Kit	Unit 3: Out of this World	Unit 4: Travellers' Tales	Unit 5: Making the News	Unit 6: Your Language
Extending and applying the grammatical knowledge set out in English Appendix 2 to the Key Stage 1 and 2 programmes of study to analyse more challenging texts	L5, L7, L9	L5, L6 (TC)	L1, L2, L4, L6	L1, L3, L4	L3	L3, L4
Studying the effectiveness and impact of the grammatical features of the texts they read	L2, L5, L6 (TC), L7, L9	L3 (TC), L5	L1, L2, L6, L7	L2, L3, L4	L3	
Drawing on new vocabulary and grammatical constructions from their reading and listening, and using these consciously in their writing and speech to achieve particular effects	L1, L5, L6, L7	L5	L2, L3, L6, L7	L1, L3, L4	L9	L4, L10
Knowing and understanding the differences between spoken and written language, including differences associated with formal and informal registers, and between Standard English and other varieties of English		L9				L1, L2, L5, L6, L7, L10
Using Standard English confidently in their own writing and speech	L8, L9	L1, L9	L5	L2, L3, L4, L8	L1, L2 (TC), L5, L9	L5, L6, L7, L10
Discussing reading, writing and spoken language with precise and confident use of linguistic and literary terminology	L5, L6, L7	L2, L4, L5, L6, L8, L9	L1, L2, L6,	L1, L3		L1, L2, L3, L4, L5, L6, L7, L10

Also available: A wealth of SPAG interactives on Kerboodle LRA 1, 2 and 3.

KS3 National Curriculum and *Ignite English* mapping: **Spoken English**

National Curriculum: subject content	Unit 1: In Search of Adventure	Unit 2: The Identity Kit	Unit 3: Out of this World	Unit 4: Travellers' Tales	Unit 5: Making the News	Unit 6: Your Language
Using Standard English confidently in a range of formal and informal contexts, including classroom discussion	L1, L2, L8	L1 (TC), L2 (TC), L3 (TC), L6 (TC), L8 (TC)	L4, L8 (TC), L9 (TC)	L1, L3, L5 (TC), L7	L1, L2, L4, L6, L8, L10	L8 (TC)
Giving short speeches and presentations, expressing their own ideas and keeping to the point			L1 (TC), L5	L4, L5, L8	L6, L7, L8, L10	L2 (TC), L5 (TC), L10
Participating in formal debates and structured discussions, summarizing and/or building on what has been said	L7 (TC), L8		L5		L2	
Improvising, rehearsing and performing play scripts and poetry in order to generate language and discuss language use and meaning, using role, intonation, tone, volume, mood, silence, stillness and action to add impact	L4	L1 (TC), L2 (TC), L5, L9	L3	L4 (TC), L5 (TC)	L7	

Key: L = Lesson (Student Book); TC = Teacher Companion